Conscious Acts of Grace

GIFTS OF LOVE AND KINDNESS AT THE END OF LIFE

by Liza Ely
Creator of "Celebration Circles"™

Giraffe Talk
Publications

Copyright (c) 2010 by Giraffe Talk Publications

All Rights Reserved. No part of this book may be reproduced in any form or by any electronic or mechanical means, including information storage and retrieval systems, without written permission, except by a reviewer who may quote passages in a review. For more information, contact Giraffe Talk Publications, P.O. Box 1421, Lindale, TX 75771.

Library of Congress Control Number: 2009911141

Cover art and cover design by Janet Brooks • www.janetbrooks.com
Author photograph by Kris Burton • www.krisburton.com
Manufactured in the United States of America

ISBN 978-0-615-32947-5

To my readers:

You are valiant and brave.
It takes courage to enter into stories about dying.
This taboo subject is usually avoided at all costs. And yet, other
than birth into our bodies, it is the one experience all humans
share. You are invited to proceed gently with an open heart,
knowing you are a pioneer in bringing death into life
and a leader in moving our culture from fear into love.
Read and listen with the assurance
you will be safe, comforted, and inspired.

Liza Ely

Contents

Introduction xv

Listening 1
   Acts of Listening 19
   Questions to Consider... 21

Support 23
   Acts of Support 39
   Questions to Consider... 40

Dignity 41
   Acts of Dignity 57
   Questions to Consider... 59

Faith 61
   Acts of Faith 74
   Questions to Consider... 75

Letting Go 77
   Acts of Letting Go 90
   Questions to Consider... 91

Forgiveness 93
   Acts of Forgiveness 102
   Questions to Consider... 104

Celebration Circles 105
   Acts of Creating a Circle 117
   Questions to Consider... 121

And Then Some 123
   Questions to Consider... 138

Dedication

I dedicate this book to my dear friend and one of the most remarkable women I have ever met, Audray Landrum.

She was grace. At her memorial service, one of her co-workers stood and said, "If Jesus had had a little sister, it would have been Audray." He said it so well!

Even during her experience of diagnosis and treatment for breast cancer, she was an inspiration to all who came in contact with her.

I share with you the last words that she left us in writing, an un-mailed letter found on her desk after her death. It was addressed to the chaplain at the hospital where she spent her last few months.

It is a reminder that conscious acts of grace can go both ways.

I share with you Audray's letter:

Dear John,

You and I shared a conversation as we sat together outside the radiation department warming our bones. That conversation - most particularly a question you posed to me - has been great fodder for my contemplation.

I don't recall precisely what led to the question. You asked how my journey of many months at the hospital is going. I responded with something about peaks and valleys. Eventually, I referenced my need to refocus on what there was for me to be grateful about. It was at this point you asked, "Does that really work for you?"

You continued, "Sometimes I'm really in a sour place and my wife yells at me to 'adopt an attitude of gratitude'!" Your pager was sounding for the third time at this point, so my parting comment as I laughed at your mimic of your wife was, "Oh well, yes, you do have to be ready to let go before gratitude has a chance."

I've reviewed that question and my answer many times since then. I've observed myself in times of fear, pain, and self-pity hanging onto those miserable enemies of all that is good. I know that all I have to do is shift my focus to a larger picture - the sky, butterflies, birdsongs, rustling leaves, the sound of laughter. I know that in the blink of an eye my perception of my situation can change dramatically. In the moment nothing has really changed for me except what I'm thinking about and focusing on. I think therein lies the primary difference between Jesus and the rest of God's children. He was always in control of his mind. He always chose God.

I sometimes choose the "brothers grim," fear, pain, self-pity, anger, et al, for my companions. Lucky for me I know, without question, that God is omnipresent and no matter where my mind wanders or where my perceived experiences take me . . . He is there. I just have to get around to remembering that and being willing to let go and to trust.

I just wanted to say thank you for inspiring me to reconsider my faith through a very important question and for always being available to share a hug, a conversation or kindness.

Hafiz is a favorite poet Saint, and I love this quote from one of his poems:

> Where is the door to God?
> In the bark of a dog?
> In the ring of a hammer?
> In the faces of Everyone I see.

It's just easier to see Him in you, my friend!

Blessings,

Audray

This book would not exist without the generous spirits and big hearts of the contributors. My eternal gratitude goes to:

GeNeil Avery

Lisa Braswell

Carrie Couture

Dianne Farrell

4Bears

Bob Hill

Barbara Hoepp

Sita Hood

Cathy Ingham

Jan King

Jeannette LaFontaine

Nanette Laney

Linda Limb

Marolen Mullinax

Jalyn Noel

Ruth Pittard

Tracey Protsman

Linda Schulz

Linda Turner

Margaret Walden

Acknowledgements

Not only does it "take a village to raise a child," it takes a village to birth a book. This would not be in your hands right now if it were not for the deep and on-going support of many.

Jim Bundscho's fingerprint is on every aspect of this book, from brainstorming ideas, content editing, copyediting, formatting, questioning, and supporting. Thank you, dear one.

I have been guided, prodded, reminded, and challenged with tenacious support by my dear friend Terrie King.

The beauty of the book was from the tremendous talents of artist Janet Brooks. I finally own a piece of your splendid art, Janet! Thank you!

Thank you Kris Burton for your artist eye, generosity, and unending encouragement.

I thank Marguerite Chandler, my "midwife," for her guidance in this birthing process. She was always available to share her insights, encouragement, and resources.

Carol Herrington questioned how I could expand on Jerry's story, thus the creation of Celebration Circles! Thank you, Carol, for this exciting expansion of action.

I give special thanks to Holly Rand, Belinda Kennedy, Dede Applegate, Ingrid Martine, Cheryl Fillion, Cheri Lambert for their editing and suggestions. I thank my copy editor, Michael Garrett for his feedback and input.

Thank you my dear brother Jim Burnett, for sharing your experiences and suggestions from your own writing and publishing process, as well as your editing suggestions. And thanks, to my "sister" Velma Burnett for your sharp eye and input.

My love to my family, James and Verna D Burnett, Deanna Bearden, and Laura and Dave McClendon for loving me and always supporting me in living my passions.

There is something magical about any intense, tightly knit group of people working together and playing together, a feeling of being in the world while at the same time being apart from it, apart together. We believe that even those of us who have not experienced that magic hear its distant music, feel its ancient call...Such a community can create the context and the confidence for a transforming journey.

~ George Leonard and Michael Murphy ~

Introduction

Graceful Transitions

Conscious acts of grace are those touches, words, and actions that let our loved ones know we are there for them at the end of their physical life. They are the acts of unselfishness, of forgiveness, of kindness, and compassion. They are the acts of highest love that allow us to release someone from our physical world, out of their pain and tiredness. They are acts of grace that allow for ease, caring, luminosity, and bliss.

Conscious acts of grace are when we move beyond the question, "What is going to happen to me when this person is gone?" Instead, we ask, "How can I best love this person?"

I have never heard anyone say that he/she wished for a painful, lingering death. In our culture we tend to go to the extremes. The miracle of Western medicine is that we can keep bodies alive even when the spirit is gone. This can also be a tremendous burden, bringing great sadness and sorrow. We often hold on, in fear, long past the time in which our body's work is done.

The other extreme is to consider assisted suicide as an option. We may even jokingly say, "If I ever get to where I can't function, just put me out of my misery." There has been much media attention, and great emotion on both sides, to this option of terminally ill medical patients being assisted with their own suicide.

Rather than rely on these extremes, we as family and friends can allow and support that which is our birthright. Just as it is natural to be born from our mother, it is just as natural to be "birthed" from our bodies.

Conscious acts of grace are the middle ground. The hospice movement has opened up the freedom and availability of this possibility. What if we could be in a place of physical and emotional peace so that we could gently release? What if we were supported and encouraged to open our hearts to healing and forgiveness? What if those we hold most dear to our hearts could be with us and be a part of this most miraculous moment?

I believe that we, as individuals, have an enormous capacity to determine when we transition out of our bodies. It is simple, yet it isn't. There are many reasons why we stay here, even if our work is done, and we say we are ready to "go." By coming from a place of compassion with our loved ones, and ourselves, we can actually move to a place of celebration and find the gifts of this season in our lives.

How often have we heard of one partner following another after a short period of time? Or, of the woman who says she wants to live until her child arrives from out of town and as the adult child arrives and says goodbye, the mother softly fades?

Historically, there are some powerful examples of just such choices. Thomas Jefferson and John Adams, framers of the Constitution and end-of-life friends and confidants, both died on July 4th, 1826, the fiftieth anniversary of the adoption of the Declaration of Independence.

Mark Twain was born on the day of Haley's Comet. He is quoted as saying, "I came in with Haley's Comet in 1835. It is coming again next year, and I expect to go out with it." He died of a heart attack on April 21, 1910, the month of Haley's return.

Noted comedian and actor George Burns declared the desire and intent to live to be 100. He died forty-nine days after his 100th birthday. As much as he looked forward to reaching 100, he also declared he was looking forward to being reunited with his beloved wife, Gracie.

One of the reasons we often "hang on" is because of the fear that we did not do everything we were supposed to do for others during our lives. We, as humans, seem to be good at remembering all of our mistakes and are often deficient in remembering the good we bring to the world. Celebration Circles bring the gift of remembering and of sharing. The honoree of the Circle is often surprised and deeply moved by hearing how their actions impacted others in a positive manner. There is a deep healing in knowing that others, and the world, are different because they existed.

How would it be for us to claim the power of our own passing? We, with the support of our loved ones, release in joy!

This understanding and way of being with others and ourselves is a personal mission for me. First and foremost, I am a human being who has and will again experience death in my life. I have personally known deep grief. I have watched as family and friends have struggled with releasing those they love, even when the time is clear or have struggled with their own death processes.

Second, I have spent the last thirty years of my life working in the field of mental health. As a professional counselor, I have been present for others as they move through their own suffering. Personally and professionally I have come to know how through the choices of our thoughts, words and actions, we can live a life of greater joy and peace. I have seen daily how our underlying belief systems, whether conscious or unconscious, determine the quality of our lives. There is good news in that awareness. If what we believe is causing us misery, we can change our minds. We can "be with" a situation in a different manner. We can make new choices.

This book is offered as a reminder of how important it is to let our loved ones go when it is time. It is a reminder that those of us left behind have loved and have been loved.

These shared stories remind us all of how to be with one another in a place of holy love. You are invited to join us on this journey of practicing conscious acts of grace.

To die will be an awfully big adventure.

~ Sir James Matthew Barrie ~

Listening

The first duty of love is to listen.

~ Paul Tillich ~

Listening. The art of listening seems to be the most difficult skill for most of us humans to learn. True listening, deep listening, listening with heart!

First, we must listen to ourselves, listen "in." This requires quietness, stillness, and openness. With our sense of urgency in today's world, we often neglect allowing the time and space for this quietness. It is listening to our dreams, in wakefulness or in sleep. It is paying attention to those messages that may come to us when our mind is still.

It is listening to our "gut feelings," to our hearts. It is easy to "intellectualize" whatever is happening in our world. When we have that sense in our gut, we may ignore it, try to make sense with only our brain, or even medicate it.

With this listening "in," we can know what it is we need to do. We can have clarity. We can take action so that we do not regret inaction.

Christmas time in Texas meant my house was filled with lively conversations, cooking, baking, present wrapping and entertaining one another. My Daddy (I was lucky to be raised by two men, my step dad and my birth Daddy) came in as planned and my in-laws had shown up unannounced as a surprise for us. My mind was buzzing with eight people in my small house, all men except for my mom-in-law and me.

I was quite distracted this holiday week with many lengthy phone calls from my mom in Missouri. Dad had been in the hospital less than a week with bronchitis and moved to ICU, as the medications were not working. Several specialists were running tests, and nothing was showing up as to why he was so ill.

Two days before Christmas a strained, high pitched voice said, "Merry Christmas, Tracey" as a chill went through my entire body.

Mom came back on the phone, and I asked, "Is he dying Mom?" Her reply confirmed my fear.

To my relief, Christmas Day passed and my company prepared to leave. I had kept the random daydreams and thoughts of Dad dying, and the sad feelings that came with them, to myself. I attempted to dismiss all of them and yet they persisted. It wasn't until my youngest son came to share with me his dream that I truly worried.

Listening

My fifteen-year old son, much like myself, has seen beyond this realm many times, is intuitive, and has had dreams come true. He shared his dream about how his grandpa had died, and everyone was acting as if nothing had happened at all. It was at that moment that I stopped, looked, listened, and suddenly trusted the symbols I was being given.

"I believe he's going to die, and no one really understands why or believes this right now. Let me know of any more dreams you have, Sweetie," I said to my son.

I began speaking my truth and told Mom my thoughts about the dream. Within a few days the conversations with Mom were becoming more surreal. It was as if I was speaking a foreign language, and yet we both understood it.

"Did Michael have any more dreams?" she asked.

"Yes, the other night," I said quietly. "He told me he dreamt that you and I were in the hospital room standing together, and Dad was dead on the hospital bed. I asked if anyone else was in the room and he said we were the only ones there, that his aunts and uncle weren't anywhere in the dream."

Next time we talked I heard myself saying to my mom: "Two ... two ... you have two days, Mom. Or two hours. Or today.

All I know for certain is 'two - two' and you need to talk to Dad in a real and deep way."

"Okay, I'll talk to him. Two, huh?" she asked tearfully.

My older sister had left to go back home to Wisconsin as the doctors assured her he was going to recover. That same day I booked my flight to Missouri, and on New Year's Eve landed at Dad's side in the hospital with my mom and my brother.

The next day one of the specialists came forward, had a heartfelt talk with us, and said that it was only the oxygen keeping him alive. We could ventilate and use life support machines, or let him go. My siblings were contacted and our choice was difficult, yet unanimous. None of us wanted him to suffer any more.

Michael's dream began to play out for us exactly as it was shown to him. Mom and I were suddenly alone in the room with Dad, on both sides of his bed, faced with a sacred responsibility. We both felt peaceful as we spoke to Dad and explained to him what was happening. For a couple of hours we nurtured his humanity, tended to his physical pain, talked to him, as well as to his Spirit. Mom waited until we both felt a warm, loving acceptance come from Dad before lifting the oxygen mask off of his face.

We were both holding Dad's hands in our own. Mom reached her arm across his body and took my hand. Her face was smiling, and tears were gently rolling down her cheeks, a mirror image of myself. We had formed a circle with our hands, and in his silence he acknowledged our presence and was deeply happy! Contrary to the doctor's words stating that the last breath would be loud and gasping, Dad's last breath was so very quiet. He died about two minutes after the oxygen was shut off as I sang to him "Amazing Grace, how sweet the sound that takes our daddy home."

I felt so incredibly honored to be there. It was as if Dad knew it needed to be just Mom and me in the room for his personal transition and for his family. So, he sent his Spirit forward to drop the gift of dreams and symbols here in Texas for my son, my Mom, and me to complete his wishes, which could not be spoken out loud.

And as for the "twos" that I saw again and again in my mind's eye and the loud "two-two" voice that yelled in my ear repeatedly, they were symbolic. Two days after I arrived and two minutes after removing the oxygen, Dad passed away on Tuesday, the second.

It is easy to discount that which is not logical. Listening to our heart messages requires being receptive and open.

Bob had a big heart and glorious laugh. I was his single, next door neighbor and we spent many hours on his porch swing. He advised me on life and love. He listened and shared stories of his long life.

With his wife having died of Alzheimer's and his only daughter living in California, Bob and I "adopted" one another. When he was in intensive care on one occasion, I told the nursing staff I was his daughter so that I could be with him and take care of his needs. He took great responsibility to make sure he could live independently, hiring help for his daily needs. Other neighbors loved and supported him as well, seeing he was safe and cared for as his health continued to fail.

Bob slowly slipped into a state of unawareness in his last hospital stay. My last visit with him was simply holding his hand and having a one-way conversation.

That night, as I slept, I was awakened with a loud request from Bob, "Wake up Liza, wake up. It is 6 AM." I immediately looked at the clock and it was in fact only 3:23 AM. I was sure it was Bob calling to me. I laid there in my bed, imagining being with him, holding his hand, talking with him with words of appreciation of all that he had brought to my world. I told him he was safe. I told him he was loved. I eventually slipped back into sleep.

First thing in the morning, I went to the hospital to Bob's room. It was empty. I went to the nurse's desk to inquire. Bob passed from his well-used body at 3:26 AM. How grateful I am that I was able to be with him in spirit during his last moments.

Listening to ourselves means an awareness of our boundaries. How do we stay in integrity with our obligations and be open to the unexpected happenings? How do we decide when and how to take action? A question I ask myself is, "Because I love me, I choose _____."

I know that I have to make my choices based on my values and the ability to discern what is most important at any given moment. **By taking that moment to truly listen to myself, the clarity and solutions to possible conflicting actions comes.**

I had just left a friend's home, on my way out of town. As I was driving down a straight stretch of the road, I saw a large golden dog struggling and moving in pain, with the bottom half of his front leg bent backwards. As I approached, I could see that he had been injured.

Having two dogs who are precious to me, I always feel a sadness in my heart when I see an animal that has been struck by a car. I have rarely seen one that is still alive and in need of attention. There were houses around him, so I guessed he lived close by. I called my friend, Jim, who lived less than a mile away, to come check on the dog and to try to locate the owner. I proceeded out of town.

I kept feeling a nagging in my stomach to go back. I struggled with my time limitations. I knew Jim would take care of matters. Yet, my "voice" kept saying to turn around. I listened and reversed direction.

By the time I was back, the dog was lying on the grass beside the road. Jim had already knocked on doors and learned that a neighbor had witnessed the hit, and the owners were not home.

The dog was in obvious pain and distress. Jim was calling different organizations, searching for assistance and options. We knew we could not lift him, due to his size and injuries. I kneeled beside the dog, talking softly and using my hands to offer healing. As more time passed, blood started dripping from his open mouth, and I knew the injuries were extremely serious.

As it became evident that death was coming, we both sat on the ground and offered comfort through our words, sounds, and touch. I remembered a speaker from hospice saying that no one should ever have to die alone.

Listening

As his breathing became labored, we assured him that he was safe. We assured him that he was not alone. When he was gone, Jim covered him with a blanket, leaving a note on the owner's door as to where he was.

I am grateful I listened to myself and turned around. Rather than being haunted with the image of the struggle of an injured living being in the road, I am left with the experience of being present and offering comfort for those last moments.

*What we have done for ourselves alone dies with us;
what we have done for others and the world remains
and is immortal.*

~ Albert Pike ~

How do we listen to others? How can we be fully present with and for our loved one? When we have already done the "listening in," we know we are respecting our own needs, and we can then listen more readily to others.

So many times, as we listen to another, we are thinking about what we want to say in response. We are just waiting for them to take a breath so that we can interject our own experience. True listening means putting our own agenda "on hold."

It just may be that the ultimate listening challenge is to have a conversation with our loved ones when they are at the end of their lives. How do we bring it up?

It may be that all that is necessary is to say, "I am here. Anything you want to talk about, I am here to listen and support." Then just listen with compassion and clarity. Tears are okay. There is no need to "fix" their fears. Just "be." Just hold their hand, and let them know they are loved.

I remember my last visit with my cousin's wife. I was in my late twenties, and she was in her early thirties. She was the new mother of a young daughter and in the last stages of breast cancer. I, too, was a young mother. I could not imagine the emotions she must have been feeling regarding leaving her baby daughter and her older son.

Listening

She was hooked up to equipment, with tubes coming in and out. She was pleasant and seemed appreciative of the visit. And yet, the "elephant was in the room," and neither of us spoke of it. I did not know what to say, beyond the surface pleasantries.

How was I to talk to her of her death? How was I to let her know it was okay to tell me anything? We had only had a casual friendship, so talking about something so intimate was scary for me. And, although this was over thirty years ago, I still remember clearly the feeling of deep sadness that I was not able to be there for her emotionally in the way I would have liked. After I left her room that night, I never saw her again.

Since then, I have learned how important it is to bring up the hard subjects. We miss the opportunity for deep connection when we, the one dying and the friend/family member, gingerly step around the obvious out of fear of offending or bringing up a subject so intimate.

The one dying may not initiate the conversation because common responses are "Don't talk like that, you're going to be just fine." Our own fears and discomforts can keep us from the most powerful experience of connection with another human being.

As I knocked and opened the door, I could already feel the change inside. Julia, who was usually stretched out in her recliner chair, was asleep in the new hospital bed that had been delivered. She looked so peaceful lying there, but it was late in the day, and she was my last visit, so I called her name. She woke easily, and we began to converse. I always asked if she had any pain, and she responded by telling me that it was all over her body. As long as she did not move, it was only a mild discomfort. The nurses believed that it was arthritic pain, and they had increased her medication. She struggled to hear me, as once again she did not have her hearing aids in.

As always, she was in her pajamas. This perfect little lady who used to style hair in her home and loved to dress for an evening out with her husband had not bothered to put clothes on for a month. She would go only from the bed, to the recliner, and to the toilet. Even in that small space, she managed to fall and spent two hours lying on the floor before anyone found her. The large rug burn could still be seen on her arm.

After small talk about her niece and the table and chairs that she would like to purchase for her dining area, I looked at this tiny china doll and asked, "Do you feel like you have one foot in heaven?" Finally, we were at the truth, the place of no return, the moment that hospice and the months of building our relationship were all about.

Listening

She told me that her prayers had changed. She no longer asked God for anything, but rather just told God that she was ready to go home. Julia talked to me about her funeral, and the single pink rose that she wished to have in her coffin from her deceased husband. She hoped that her niece would give her tea roses rather than a big, fussy flower display, but she did not want to tell her that. I decided not to tell her either, when I called later to check in.

Julia had planned every detail of her funeral including the song, "You'll Never Walk Alone," which I sang for her and told her that she shouldn't have to wait until she's gone to hear it. We talked about the funeral as if she would be there, and she invited me to be a guest. I don't go to many funerals anymore but believe that I will make Julia's.

She told me about the gown that a friend was dressed in for her funeral and how she decided she wanted the same, but in pink. She ordered it, and we both knew that it would be beautiful. She was like a little girl, sharing her plans with me and explained that none of her friends in the community would allow her to discuss these details. They would all laugh at her and put her off, telling her that it was too depressing.

I have reviewed hundreds of living wills and "do not resuscitate" orders with my residents, so this is nothing new for me. Before I left Julia, I sat on the bed and kissed and hugged her several times, stating the possibility that this might be the last time we were together. She kept thanking me for letting her talk about these important plans. This is what I do. I listen. I let people tell me the things that no one else is comfortable hearing. And what effect does it have on me? I still fight the urge to run. No matter how comfortable I become with secrets, there is a part of my own psyche that doesn't want to know. Julia never knew this.

Sometimes we may think that the time for listening has passed, that it is too late. We may ignore or discount possible opportunities for a final connection with our loved one. These opportunities may be fragile and fleeting. By being fully in the moment, we may receive the gift of the unexpected for one final moment of joy.

Grandpa's hands played with my necklace a lot and stared at the stone in the pendant. He said lots of sentences that sounded like gibberish to me as he looked at the shiny silver. Once in a while he stopped, looked at me and realized who I was. His eyes beamed with light and love, and he would grin, saying, "Ahhh daughter, look what beauty God has brought me." Just as quickly, his Spirit would pull him away, and my Grandpa seemed to leave, just pop out to that space and place where dreams begin . . . into another realm.

My grandpa had been made comfortable in his home for the last three weeks of his life with the aid of hospice and the love of his large family. During these last few weeks he was not present enough to carry on a conversation and offered only a sentence or two. He was easily confused and forgot where he was and who he was with. It was so hard for my grandma and his six daughters to see him lingering here like this. They talked to him as if he were a child. Their tears flowed when occasionally he popped back in his body and was aware of those around him and graced them with his smile and phrases of love. His face would light up, and he would say something beautiful to Grandma or to those of us visiting or caring for him.

I watched him as he twirled his fingers around my necklace chain and just knew he would come "present" for me on this visit, our last visit here on earth. We had always shared a special spiritual connection. I waited patiently, watching him and talking to him.

I told him I was here and requested his Spirit come back to me so that we could speak.

Suddenly, he put the palm of his hand on my forehead and just stared at me in silence. As I put my hand on his forehead, we just looked deeply for the longest time at one another. I knew he was coming through to talk to me again. He had such a smile on his face and he seemed to glow.

He began talking to me, and he was as clear as he had been months ago. He told me that he was glad my mom had come to visit because now all of his girls had been to see him that day. His hand still on my face, he said that I was his daughter, too, and how blessed he felt that I had come to show him my colors. He asked about my three boys, and we talked about Eric having visions and dreams that come true. He told me he would try to keep the promise he made to me three years ago that if he were allowed to do so when he left this plane that he would communicate with me from Spirit. And so warmly, Grandpa began telling me more about how special I have always been to him and how he was so blessed with my being in his life.

Suddenly, he looked puzzled and said he wished he could see my friend as well. He couldn't think of her name, so I asked, "Margaret?"

Listening

He said, "Yes, Margaret," and told me to tell her that he loved her. I told him I could get her on the phone for him to talk to. He was so surprised his eyes widened as he asked, "You can?"

I said, "Yes, I have my cell phone."

He asked, "Would you mind? Would it be too much trouble?"

I said, "No, not at all. But you must stay present while I get her on the phone. Stay with me now, don't leave, okay?"

I got the phone and dialed quickly, getting Margaret on the speaker phone as fast as I could. He was able to hear her voice and tell her how much he cared for her and what a beautiful friendship the two of us shared.

I sat the phone in my lap and focused on Grandpa. His hand continued to stroke my face and mine lay on his. I imagined that we both were glowing from this beautiful interaction we were sharing. What moments these were! He was present of mind and with me in our little space of time for at least ten minutes, fully coherent!

He assured me in a strong tone that he would continue his work with God after he died and that if "They" allowed, he would visit me soon. I leaned over his bed, kissed his head, and said "Grandpa, it's time to go home. It's time to go home."

He said, "Yes, Sugar, it is. It is." He kissed and kissed my smiling, teary face and gently Spirit took him back to that haven of in between here and there.

He became confused again and began to babble, wanting someone, pointing in mid air with his finger. I asked if he was in pain and he said, "Yes." He said, "Get the person." I left his room and told my aunt that he needed some medicine.

I drove Mom back home soon after my visit with Grandpa. I left with an overwhelming sadness that equaled my gratitude for his efforts and ability to be present with me one last time.

Deep listening is miraculous for both listener and speaker.
When someone receives us with open-hearted, non-judging,
intensely interested listening, our spirits expand.

~ Sue Patton Thoele ~

Acts of Listening:

Create a fifteen minute break for yourself, away from others and tasks. Take a walk, sit quietly, and close your eyes. Just allow your thoughts to come and go, without any particular agenda. Allow for stillness.

❧

When faced with a decision, stop and breathe. Listen "in." Notice those thoughts that float in. Pay attention to yourself. Listen to the "arguments" within your head and heart and ask, "What do I need to make this the best possible decision?" Notice what you are feeling. How can you provide that need for yourself?

❧

Ask for listening from others when needed.

❧

Practice in "easy" situations. Initiate a conversation in which you ask someone questions. Face him/her softly, with eye contact. Keep your focus on the person in front of you, ignoring possible distractions. Give feedback about what you are hearing, without getting into your own "story."

൞

Avoid arguing with their reality and instead ask, "What do you need right now?" Listen to their answer with your heart. Give feedback on the emotion, without trying to "fix" the situation for them.

൞

When visiting someone ill, sit quietly by their bedside and just take their hand. Allow them to direct the subject of the conversation. Allow for long pauses, knowing that what comes next is often profound.

൞

Listening

Questions to Consider:

Remember back to a time when you felt someone truly listened to you. What did it look like? What did it sound like? What did it feel like?

☙

In what ways can you make the time and space to be sure that you are listening to yourself,
acknowledging your own needs and desires?

☙

When was a time you listened to your own inner voice, your "gut" feeling? What happened?

☙

When was a time you did not listen to your own inner voice? What happened?

☙

When was a time in which you truly listened to another? What did it feel like? What did you do to make it happen?

☙

How can you best remember to be a listener for yourself?

☙

How can you best remember to be a listener for others?

☙

Support

Oh, the comfort, the inexpressible comfort of feeling safe with a person; having neither to weigh thoughts nor measure words, but to pour them all out, just as they are, chaff and grain together, knowing that a faithful hand will take and sift them, keep what is worth keeping, and then, with a breath of kindness, blow the rest away.

~ George Eliot ~

My beloved husband, Austin, almost died twice before he actually did. The first time was a year after we married. I realized I had done what many women do and had put all of my time and focus on our relationship. I was relying on him for all of my social needs. He provided me with emotional support and a listening heart. He would challenge me emotionally, providing reality testing. He was a great playmate. He was there for me in times of physical need, from illness to a flat tire. He would brainstorm with me as I planned workshops and edited my writing. He supported my spiritual growth. My needs were met, so why spend time elsewhere?

With his first dramatic illness, I became acutely aware that "all of my eggs were in one basket." I knew that I needed to reconnect with other friends and become more active socially. Sometimes he participated with me, and sometimes I acted alone. I will be eternally grateful for the opportunity I had to experience a "dry run" of him no longer being in my life.

Many years later, a neighbor heard my wailing when I discovered my husband's body. She asked whom she should call. I gave her a name and phone number, and within an hour, a room full of compassionate and caring friends surrounded me. I looked up from my phone conversation with Austin's daughter and they were literally encircling me. I called them my human hula-hoop. They continued to surround me in spirit and support as I moved through that tortuous recovery process.

Their support took many forms. Sometimes it was as simple as asking, "Where is your broom?" and sweeping up the accumulated leaves on the deck. Or, "What phone calls can I make for you?" It was as moving as an invitation to lie on the couch and be sung to, while I was given a gentle foot massage. It was as touching as sitting on the floor with me while joining me in crying.

Being supported means asking for what we need. It means being willing to receive the love and support from others. It means being discerning in knowing who to call upon for the desired need. Most importantly, it means being there for others.

Support can be simple and playful. It does not have to take lots of time or money. It just takes an awareness of those opportune moments.

It took quite a bit of hard work for the hospice nurse to convince these sisters that a social worker needed to begin visiting. They were three women who had lived together their entire lives. The oldest sister, Sarah, controlled the conversation and the purse strings. She liked being the decision maker and was uncomfortable with strangers in their home. At ninety-one, it was understandable that, now that they were losing one of the twins, they needed more medical attention.

As the second social worker visiting the "girls," I was on my best behavior. You couldn't see my white gloves, but trust me I was wearing them. Listening carefully to every sentence spoken, I jumped in on as many shared areas as possible. I accepted the time that they set since it didn't interfere with their afternoon nap, and I made it a point to be punctual and not tire the sisters.

Working to give attention to all, it became readily apparent that Sarah needed to be the center of everything. However, it was Emma who was losing her twin sister. She kept her tears hidden through the first visit but when I arrived for the second, they had already started. It was difficult for her to share her feelings as her older sister kept trying to stop our conversation. Of course, as the eldest, it was torture for her to think that a younger sibling was dying. Naturally, this meant that she was next. However, she sure didn't feel or look like she was planning to go anywhere soon. So, we reminisced.

For women over eighty, the beauty is often in remembering what has passed, and these two sisters were practically smacking their lips as they recounted for me the tales of their visits to Kessel's ice cream parlor where people stood in line to get a cone of Breyer's ice cream. It was all I could do to sit and listen as any story related to Breyer's was close to my heart. We were all Philly girls and, for us, this was the ice cream of choice. I knew when I left what had to be done. Searching the grocery store ads the next day, I found Breyer's on a "buy one, get one" sale. I couldn't travel with this purchase, so I chose to pick up the ice cream a week later just minutes before my visit.

As soon as I knocked on the door they were ready for me. "Didn't you get our message? We have had too many guests today. We must cancel the visit." I wasn't worried as my trip would not be in vain. Raising my arm, I announced the treat waiting for them nestled in the grocery store plastic sack, vanilla and chocolate and a second half-gallon of peach. We all shrieked because peach is never available this early in the season. Quickly, Sarah took the bag and began spooning out portions to fit the sweet little bowls that she normally only shared with her sisters. The home health aide sat to receive hers. The sisters were happy to partake and, just for this once, I chose to enjoy watching rather than eating.

We all quickly moved into a party atmosphere, and the silly stories began. I progressed into my little comedy routine about my mother's last request, a luncheon at Fisher's on Street Road with prime rib and unlimited Manhattans. She jokingly asked we sit her up in her casket as her breasts had enlarged late in life and she wanted to be sure that everyone noticed. The sisters loved this story, and of course, Sarah made a point of showing me how much she, too, had grown. This led them to talk about clothing to lay their sister out in when the time came, and I insisted to Sarah that she wouldn't have to worry as I was going to find a blue gown for her sister that would match her eyes.

They still feared their sister's death, and it will be an extremely sad moment for her twin sister. But along with the sadness will be a memory of laughter and joking about what to wear chased by a cold dish of Breyer's ice cream and that moment of sweetness.

Support may be directly related to our skills. If we have particular knowledge or experience, we may be able to offer a service or kindness that is unique.

A friend and fellow massage therapist, Sharon, kept me informed about her mother who had terminal cancer. She worried about her end of life struggles, about dying, and the state of her soul. Her mother was frightened and thought that she had not been good enough to go to Heaven. Sharon's reassurances seemed only to further agitate her. I asked Sharon to let me know if I could do anything to help.

Early one Saturday morning Sharon sent me an email with the news that her mother was actively dying. She perceived a window of opportunity for her mother to let go. Her stepfather, who was in strong denial, had left for the morning. Sharon asked me to come to the house to assist in her mother's transition. Two days before, I had been moved to cancel an appointment for this morning.

When I arrived, Sharon's mother was conscious, alert to her surroundings, but nonverbal. She was breathing quietly. Sharon introduced me, and I told her I would like to say some prayers and send her energy. I knelt at her feet, said several prayers, one of which asked for assistance from Jesus and the angels for her to walk through the door to God. Then I touched the soles of her feet. She

Support

began a death rattle, five breaths, and she was gone. Sharon was there and was aware of how easy the transition had been for her mother.

I was grateful to have been included in this sacred time, to be there for my friend as one door closed and another opened. There was such perfection in the synchronicity of the events.

It is never death because they live in your heart forever.

~ Lauren ~

The needs at end-of-life may seem overwhelming. It is a time to reach out to others, including medical, legal, and financial experts. We often procrastinate because it is a difficult topic. We don't want to offend or scare. We don't want to appear thoughtless or callous. However, planning ahead can relieve the unspoken fears. And sometimes when that isn't feasible, we must find the best possible solutions.

I was taught in nursing school the importance of sharing what you appreciate about and to others. This expression becomes even more important on the day of your loved one's death. And who can predict at what point it will be, as crystal balls are not regularly passed out. As a result, I learned to say "I love you" on a regular basis to those dear to me.

My grandfather was gentle. When I was a little girl, he let me drive his riding mower (without the blade going), and shared his love for freshly grown tomatoes and yellow raspberries. He loved to tease, then say he was just "spoofing." He laughed when I became strong enough to lift him straight into the air. He was bald for as long as I could remember, and I would kiss his head and call it his 'romantic' bald spot. Amazingly, he once let me crack an egg over it.

Upon grandpa's severe mental decline, I visited Grandma who was in distress regarding her finances. He had always handled them, and she was sure she needed to sell some stock to survive the next bout of bills. She was overwhelmed with what to do, how to get around, and who to speak with. She did not even drive. Although only twenty-two, I knew I had knowledge that would help. We went to the bank, the lawyer, and the stockbroker and did all the nitpicky, red tape, hoop-jumping and just needed Grandpa's signature on a power of attorney form.

Grandpa was smiling and asked who the young man was (pointing to me). Great, he had no idea who I was. We hugged, and I tried to explain. Tears welled. It was clear he was unable to understand what was necessary. We needed a witnessed signature. After trying to explain, and giving him a pen, he looked confused and touched the pen to the paper. Nothing. Several minutes of encouragement offered no resolution.

It occurred to me that he couldn't remember how to write, or maybe even his name. With hot waterfalls gushing down my cheeks, I took his hand in mine and formed his name to the paper. Somehow, this didn't feel right. It felt like a far cry from informed consent. I expressed to Grandma how uneasy I felt. She said, "Oh, but dear, he trusts you!"

Conscious Acts of Grace

I knew I'd never see grandpa alive again. I shared some of my best memories with him and told him I loved him, kissing his romantic bald spot tenderly. I'm not sure who helped whom the most that day. It was a day of memories, of trust, love, and the ability to help.

*Community. Somewhere, there are people to whom we can speak
with passion without having the words catch in our throats.
Somewhere a circle of hands will open to receive us,
eyes will light up as we enter, voices will celebrate with us
whenever we come into our own power.
Community means strength that joins our strength
to do the work that needs to be done.
Arms to hold us when we falter.
A circle of healing. A circle of friends.
A place where we can be free.*

~ Starhawk ~

With conscious action and creativity, our support can endure well past our physical contact. Sometimes the one dying offers the support, finding ways to remind those left behind of continuing love.

I am so grateful my son Michael and I had both made conscious choices to make beautiful memories during his earthly life.

Knowing he had a fatal disease, Michael and his sweetheart made a beautiful purple and gold quilt to give me one Christmas. My spirit is nurtured when I watch the video they made for me of the fun-filled day they drove to the special quilt store, chose each piece of cloth, drove home, started creating the pattern and sewing the pieces together. That creation room was off limits to me during several of my visits, since the evidence of this large gift of love being birthed took up much of the room. Looking back, I can still hear them giggling behind the door as they were hand sewing late into the night, thinking I was sleeping. Now, fourteen years later, it continues to warm my heart and body.

Remembering the support of others, we can pass on the kindness. We can also be kind to ourselves by creating an environment of comforting thoughts and reminders.

*M*ichael sent me a "Bird of Paradise" flower arrangement each year on Mother's Day. After my own mother passed on, I "Pay it forward" by sending a Bird of Paradise to another mother whose child has passed on. On a spiritual level, the Bird of Paradise teaches us to let go of limiting beliefs, to explore, and to be open.

At times now, when I hurt because I remember the pain my son experienced, I go to the writing that Michael communicated to me. His words, "Mom, I want you to know that what happened to me was for my own spiritual growth. Sometimes the soul needs to experience something to round out and balance the life force it's using."

I find healing and know that it is time to once again "Dance in the Rain," so I put on one of Michael's favorite Garth Brooks songs "The Dance" and am reminded that if I missed the pain, I would have missed the dance.

I dance a sacred dance of life and see Michael's precious face smiling and hear his words, "You go, Mom!"

Laughter is healing, physically and emotionally! Support can be fun and playful.

Support

My mother-in-law was a spectacular human being with a wonderful sense of humor. She spent over thirty-five years in Al-Anon and was a loving and compassionate soul. After a silent heart attack in her eighties, she was in the hospital dying.

Her room was filled with the voice of Alexander Scorsby reading the Bible on tape and the sweet voices of her friends singing. She was unresponsive for hours and sometimes days at a time. Then, out of the blue and with eyes closed, she would periodically clearly comment on something someone across the room had said. Even in dying, she had hearing like a bat!

Several days before she died, one of her sons was sitting with her and holding her hand. She tried to open her eyes, then closed them and in a mock British accent said, "I'm not dead yet!"

Without skipping a beat, the son, in his own mock British accent countered, "Yes, Mummy, but you're mostly dead."

After a few minutes, with her eyes still closed and smiling broadly she said, "Yes, but I'm feeling much better!"

(Their family had lived in England for several years and dearly loved Monty Python. The exchange between mother and son was from the "Bring Out Your Dead" scene of the Monty Python movie *Quest For the Holy Grail*.)

A few days later, just about dawn, two of her sons and I were sitting with her. One was telling her to go to her favorite place on the farm where she had grown up. He described the place, the color of the sky, the white clouds, the sounds of the birds, the trees, the view from that little hill, the smell of the air, and the feeling of the sun on her skin. He told her that she might want to spread a blanket and take a nice nap in the sun with the cool breeze on her skin.

As I looked down at her, I noticed she wasn't breathing. I kept expecting her to take another breath as she had been doing for days. After a few minutes, I looked at my watch to time her silence. One minute, two minutes, three minutes. I looked at her two sons and gently said that we were done. One of the boys said, "She's never done anything we suggested before! Go figure!"

We sat with her for a while as the sun came up and the rest of the family arrived to spend time and say their final goodbyes. There was some debate as to what would be engraved on her headstone and I still think she would have preferred, "But I am feeling much better."

*Every man goes down to his death bearing in his hands
only that which he has given away.*

~ Persian Proverb ~

Some of the most devastating places and situations, where there is deep suffering, can unexpectedly bring us life-changing beauty.

*H*er name was Guilsacen. I found her in 1991 in a rusty, peeling crib in the AIDS ward of a contagious disease hospital in Constanta, Romania. She was two years old and weighed fifteen pounds, less than my Texas cat. Our eyes met, and we saw each other.

During the next three years, "Guilsey" learned to eat, play, laugh, run, and love. She was an amazing sight with her flashing black eyes and striking gypsy beauty. Then, she began to waste away with AIDS. There was nothing to do except love her and guide her through the process. She became a little old lady. Her once soft skin stretched tight over fragile bones. Her pain was fierce, but she fought on. Her little mouth was a gaping sore of thrush and herpes, but on the good days, she still smiled.

The time came to let her go. I was too afraid to say the words out loud, but I spoke to her with my heart. Go little girl. Go to that place of peace where there is no pain and children don't have AIDS. She heard me with her heart. She was awake until the end. Guilsey died in my arms in June of 1994. What a kid!

Acts of Support:

Actively participate in groups and situations with like-minded people: a faith group, an outdoor adventure group, an environmental group, a choir, etc.

☙

Be a friend to others, call, invite, listen.

☙

When someone says, "Let's get together," ask when and make specific plans.

☙

Visit your loved one. Take him/her out for a meal or event, if he/she is mobile.

☙

Call regularly.

☙

Send cards and notes of care and concern.

☙

Let others know of desires and needs and ask for help.

☙

Tell your loved one what he/she means to you.

☙

Support

Questions to Consider:

Who will support me during my grief process?

ॐ

If I can't think of more than one or two people,
how can I expand my support system?

ॐ

In what ways do I support others?

ॐ

How do I ask for what I need?

ॐ

How do I encourage others to ask for what they need?

ॐ

Do I have specific skills that can be of use?

ॐ

Dignity

When you were born, you cried and the world rejoiced.
Live your life so that when you die, the world cries and you rejoice.

~ Indian saying ~

When raising my daughters, I made a deliberate decision to let them make the age-appropriate decisions that would not hurt them or someone else. I wanted them to discover their own needs and desires and to have freedom of expression. My belief was they would then be internally driven in their choices rather than be unduly influenced by others. As they are both happy, healthy, and successful adults, it seems to have worked well.

I have tried to remember to always use that same philosophy with those in my life who are elderly. Some decisions may not be wise to leave to their discretion, especially if dementia is present. Driving is a major one, as it can impact others in a powerful way. And yet, there are many everyday decisions that can be left up to them that will cause no harm. Like with children, it may mean taking more time and effort

Yet, it affords a sense of ownership for one's own life at a time when so many other choices are no longer present or possible.

Affording other's dignity may mean putting our own agenda on hold. It may mean keeping our mouth shut and staying away from judgment. Our greatest choice is to just love them where they are.

My grandmother, Fannie, was always stubborn. She was the eldest of ten and the only girl. Although a tough-as-nails full-blooded Indian, she allowed her soft side to show when it came to her grandchildren. MaMa married an Irishman and had two daughters. She never recovered from the unfairness of one of them dying before she did. She had always been healthy and as strong as a horse. She outlived her husband of sixty-odd years and lived on her own until she broke her hip at the age of eighty-two, falling from a ladder while trimming a tree in her backyard. They put her back together but told her she would never walk again. She showed them! Not as steady as she had been, she stumbled and hurt her ankle at age eighty-five. Without adequate circulation it just would not heal.

MaMa lived with her daughter, my mom, and me for a while but required more and more attention as her mind started to become fuzzy. She would forget and leave the stove on under an empty pan, or she would wander outside and get lost. Finally mom made the difficult decision to put her in a nursing facility. Even though Mom went to see her every day and we all went on the weekends, MaMa hated her new living arrangements. She got bedsores, no matter how much we tried to prevent it, and she just kept slipping away from us. Sometimes she didn't even know who we were when we would come and visit. Somehow, however, she always recognized the great-grandbabies!

When she was eighty-nine, my mom and I had gone to visit one Sunday, and MaMa was very lucid and sharp minded. It was a wonderful visit, and she talked about her life and how full it had been. We laughed and ate together. It was grand. She told us how much she loved us and said that she now needed us to love her more than we ever had before. She told us that PaPa (my grandfather) had come to see her the night before and had told her it was time for her to come to him. She said that she intended to do just that. She informed my mother that she was going to quit eating and that she did not want her to let the staff put a tube down her to force feed her and keep her alive.

MaMa was very bright eyed and said that she knew exactly what she was doing, and it was what she wanted more than anything. She wanted us to respect her decision and let her die with dignity, the way she wanted to die. She reminded us that her people, the

Native Americans, always knew when their time had come and would go off into the wilderness alone to die. She said that she knew that was not possible, but she wanted us to respect her wishes.

My mother and I tried to talk her out of it. My sister was pregnant, and we tried to get her excited about seeing that baby before she left us. We pleaded and cajoled, but nothing changed her mind. After a week, the staff called my mother and said they wanted to use extreme measures to feed MaMa. My mother said we would be right there.

When we arrived at the nursing facility they had everything ready to put the tube down my grandmother's throat. She lay there with those blue eyes steeled against what was about to happen. My mother asked everyone to leave the room and shut the door. She asked my grandmother one last time if this was really what she wanted and her answer was unwavering. "Yes!" My mother and I cried, and MaMa consoled us. She was already very weak from not eating, but she was firm in her resolve. She told us that she loved us and understood how hard it was to abide by her wishes, but abide we must.

When we came out of the room, they were waiting. Nurses, doctors and aides, all ready to save MaMa from herself. It was my mother's turn to be strong and stubborn. She would not give them permission to force feed MaMa. They pressured, threatened and begged. They told my mother that MaMa was not in her right mind or she would not have made such a decision. My mother stood her ground, knowing that she was battling for what my grandmother wanted, the right to decide her own fate. She wanted the right to die when and how she chose. We had already talked about it not being easy to die by starvation and my grandmother said not to worry, she would be fine.

She decided, no one else. She was so grateful to my mother, she cried and took my mom into her arms and told her that she had given her the greatest gift of all, the choice to die with honor and dignity, surrounded by love.

Sometimes, knowing we will miss someone, we forget how to let him/her go with dignity. We need one another to remind us and to love us through the hard choices.

It has become my mission to help people transition, dying from their bodies. My grandmother was critically ill after having suffered for many years with a fatal illness. Although there were no options left, my uncle wanted to hang on to any glimpse of hope. The medical professionals were clear her condition was terminal, but he could not let go and could not see past his own fears to recall her specific wishes about her death.

We found ourselves in a struggle of wills, his to hang on to her, and hers to not let go because she wanted to protect her son from the pain. The stress was taking its toll on the entire family, and as we talked through the matter, I encouraged him to give her "permission" to let go. It took several hours, but the family finally decided to stop the unnecessary medical measures to prolong her time, which were quite painful and disruptive.

Graciously, the hospital gave us a private room with unrestricted visitation. Although the physicians explained she would not last more than a few short hours, it was over forty-eight hours later when she passed on. She was semi-conscious, but clearly understood there were specific family members who had not arrived to say goodbye, so she waited for them. Also, her birthday was during the second day and she was determined to celebrate her eighty-fifth birthday with a party. My cousin fixed her hair, painted her nails and put make-up on her. We had balloons, cake, presents and lots of laughter. Shortly after midnight, she went into a coma and left us a few hours later. Her son was with her the entire time and has since spoken of those days as a beautiful time and how grateful he was to share this experience with the family.

Last year I was offered the opportunity to counsel residents in a skilled nursing facility. At first I declined, then realized I was being given an opportunity to spend time with and learn from folks who may be at the end of their lives.

What I witnessed the most is the lack of dignity afforded those in this situation and in this season of their life. They no longer have privacy. They no longer can go outside unattended. They lose their right and ability to drive and the freedoms that go along with their mobility. They have no choice regarding their food unless they are fortunate enough to have someone buy them "treats." They are surrounded by the noise of TVs, radios, intercoms, floor polishers, and trays going up and down the hall. Their bodies may be pushed and prodded and rolled down the hall to the shower, barely covered with a sheet. They are physically exposed to a staff that is ever changing, overworked, and underpaid.

Where is the dignity? Where are the choices?

Genitals on the Fritz

As we move forward into our sunset years, our genitals are handled more often by nurses than a loved one or ourselves. They wipe us, dry us, diaper us and check for problems. The slightest infection, redness or discharge and our genitals become the topic of discussion in the nursing home morning report. After all those years of being told that these were private parts, "cover yourself," "do that in your room, not in public," we are suddenly exposed to the world.

Our source of great pleasure can become a cradle of pain. Our genitals go on the fritz. Family is notified, aides are advised, lotions and potions are applied. What once was personal, special and private becomes just another body part.

The reality is that there are times our physical choices are limited. That is when we can ask ourselves what choices are still available? How can we remind one another, through listening and support, to be aware of opportunities to honor dignity?

I once read of an eighty-three year old physician who made a conscious decision to die with dignity, faith, and strength. Because of his profession, he had witnessed the "disturbing trend" of death becoming a painful and extended ordeal of medical intervention to futilely prevent the inevitable. He saw the emotional cost and suffering on the families. He was clear he wanted a different experience for himself and his family.

When the time came, he stopped eating and drinking. His wife, children and their spouses were at his bedside within

twenty-four hours, holding hands, laughing, and crying. The last two days of his life were spent sharing family stories.

No agonizing decisions about medical intervention had to be made. He had made them all for them. He knew he wanted to spend his last days in his own home, in his own bed, surrounded by the love of his family.

*M*y friend knew he was dying a slow, wasting disease and wanted to find a better way to die. He did not want to die struggling, drugged, or suffering, so he set out to find a way to let go into death consciously and joyfully. He wanted to learn to let go, to surrender with ease and grace. He traveled a lot, spending a great deal of time alone in rural settings, camping and fishing and doing the things that fed his soul. He studied indigenous people and cultures that have a different relationship with death.

In a quest for his life to be as complete as possible, he traveled to several faraway places he had always wanted to go, wrote letters to his unborn grandchildren and reviewed his life to make amends to clear his slate. He wanted to be able to open his arms to death and release his body in a way our culture does not know.

He spent over a year and a half researching and learning. One morning, he woke up and told his wife, "I think I can do this today."

His wife got up, showered and had breakfast while he stayed in bed. He began to consciously let go around 7:30 AM. Almost three hours later he became frustrated and told his wife, "This is too hard." Then, several breaths later, he was free.

This wise man left with no drugs, total consciousness, and glowing in love and excitement.

To die proudly when it is no longer possible to live proudly.
Death of one's own free choice, death at the proper time,
with a clear head and with joyfulness,
consummated in the midst of children and witnesses:
so that an actual leave-taking is possible
while he who is leaving is still there.

~ Friedrich Nietzsche ~

Sometimes we think we are doing just the "right" thing, and we are welcomed with a surprise. Understanding that medicine is an art and being flexible can help us be with the unknown with greater ease.

*T*he phone ringing at 7AM startled me out of my light sleep. The day before had presented plenty of familiar, yet distressing challenges. Mom was "coming back" to reality, now able to eat her dinner when I left the hospital the evening before. I braced myself in apprehension when the woman asked for me by my full name.

"Mrs. Couture, your mother has been transferred to ICU. She had her 7 AM dose of liquid medication and inhaled it into her lungs. We've called in the hospital respiratory specialist and her personal doctor," she explained.

The day before began with a phone call from the assisted living facility where my mother resided. They found her on the floor, staring blankly, semi-dressed, unable to get up or recognize them or where she was. These episodes were not uncommon. She suffered from cirrhosis of the liver, which resulted in elevated ammonia levels in her blood that affected brain function. The dementia that resulted was always followed by a short hospital stay, which was the only way they could administer the heavy dose of the medication.

The turn of events this morning put us on a whole new course. I was quick to understand how critical the situation at hand was due to my mother's other health problem, emphysema. This condition impaired her lung function, and she had been on oxygen for the past several years.

I was grateful for her personal doctor. Her immediate reaction was to order her to be put on antibiotic treatment to fight infection that could develop into pneumonia. She was also familiar with my mother's propensity to fight back, knowing she had experienced several miraculous comebacks, despite the test tube analysis of her conditions. Definitely a tough specimen from hardy stock, my mother had outlived her previous doctors' prognosis by several years.

The respiratory specialist and the accompanying kidney doctor met my sister and me outside my mother's room. They advised us that her lungs were not strong enough to survive this ordeal, and her kidneys were also shutting down. If by chance she did come out of this, she would be on dialysis the rest of her life. They gave her twelve to twenty-four hours to live. The shock of such a sudden turn of events was beginning to hit me. Even though you think you are prepared, you're not really ready for a final diagnosis.

My brother flew in from Virginia that night. We all gathered in her room the next morning to continue the vigil. I had even brought a CD player with her favorite Elvis tunes. I once read that listening to favorite music helps a person in their transition.

We had just turned on the music when my mother's doctor came in making her early morning rounds. She reached for her chart and began quickly scanning the data.

She reported aloud and in perfect hearing of my mother's ear, (who appeared to be asleep or unconscious), "This woman is going to be just fine. I've seen her much sicker than this, and she made a miraculous recovery." She held my mother's hand as always when talking with her. Her eyes shone bright with a knowing smile as she proclaimed this morning's revelation to us. She added that our mother was dehydrated, which gave the doctors the impression her kidneys were shutting down. All she needed was a lot of fluid for the next forty-eight hours.

The doctor had not been gone three minutes when my mother opened her eyes and proclaimed, "Get this thing off my face and turn that music off. I'm not going anywhere yet! And get me something to drink, will you? I'm so thirsty!"

My mother lived another year and a half. This episode gave my sister, brother and me many a good laugh and fond memories of our invincible heritage.

We can be inspired by the dignity of the dying. We can listen and learn.

*E*leanor walked in the company of cancer, but she gave it no prestige. When her hair fell out, she plunked on a baseball cap. If her energy got zapped, she came to group in her pajamas.

No complaints, no pleas for sympathy; only a quiet dignity, which spoke volumes about the woman she really was.

Eleanor was a weaver. At times she used words to captivate the group, stringing together sentences, creating stories from her heart. Other times she used chenille, silk, wool and sometimes beads, producing scarves for public consumption. They were soft, but sturdy, colors that attracted comment and threads that made a body feel comforted.

Eleanor was a presence in our company of women writers. She was a force in the community and a mother of eight children. But most importantly, through her open heart and incredible energy, Eleanor twinkled.

She lit up the room with her twinkle. She touched hearts with her twinkle. She met death with her twinkle.

It was a merry light, coming straight through her eyes from her soul. It touched my heart to be included in that twinkle. Like her story about umbrellas, it was a twinkle I shall never forget. It was a twinkle that said come closer, share a bit of yourself. Stop worrying. Enjoy!

We can look for all possible opportunities to provide options for dignity. Talk with others who have been through similar circumstances. Talk with experts, such as staff at the

Dignity

Alzheimer's Association. Brainstorm ... and always remember to include the person involved to the highest possible level.

A woman who was the mother of one of my childhood friends had a small stroke and then began to show signs of dementia. She was in her mid-eighties and otherwise was in good health. At first, she tried staying on her own, but it proved to be too difficult. Her "tracker" was broken, and she couldn't remember if she had eaten or taken her medicine. It was decided she would live with one of her daughters.

In spite of the wonderful care she received, these new living arrangements didn't work. She felt awkward, like a burden, and longed for the familiarity of her own home and routine. Her children had a family meeting and decided to hire live-in care so she could stay in her own home. She was excited to return home to her house, dog, and land!

With her caretaker, she could resume her routine of taking walks down the driveway to the mailbox (about 1/4 mile each way), listening to music and sitting outside to enjoy her koi pond and the beauty of surrounding woods. Her friends came to visit, read to her, sang with her or took her out for a drive. She continued to have periodic small strokes and began to gradually slip away.

I gave her weekly massages, and she would talk to me almost the whole time. She spoke of her choice to approach dementia with open arms and curiosity. Fear, she explained, was optional and it didn't seem to serve her well. Again and again she spoke of her enormous gratitude for her children who were loving her and "holding the space" while she "lost her mind." Gradually, her walks became shorter and shorter, then they ceased all together. She still loved to sit out in her yard, watching the birds at the feeder with childlike wonder. Her once razor-sharp mind would slip in and out of "gear" for longer periods of time. Words began to fail. And finally, she was bedridden, unable to make words at all.

During visits, I would hold her hand. When she would struggle to make herself understood, I would tell her that we could just "be" together and communicate with our hearts. We didn't need words. Once in a while she would say something clear as a bell. But mostly she would sleep. Her family and friends were with her around the clock. Towards the end, someone slept in the room with her because she would wake up late at night and be scared and disoriented. All it took was a reassuring hand on her arm, and she would faintly smile and drift off. She was in bed a little over a month before she was able to gently let go late one night.

Acts of Dignity:

Remember to listen to what the other is requesting and ask, "What do you need right now?"

❧

Notice all opportunities to provide privacy for your loved one.

❧

Requests from loved ones may be unrealistic or unreasonable such as, "I want to leave this hospital now." Acknowledge their pain and distress, without trying to be logical and sensible with them. "I know this must be difficult to be stuck in this bed, away from your home."

❧

Remind them of what they can still do: "Would you like to get in your wheelchair and go outside for awhile?"

❧

Ask for their input on decisions that are reasonable for their participation.

❧

Ask for their opinion in areas of their knowledge and expertise.

☙

When in the presence of medical personnel / staff / friends and your loved one, include him/her in the conversation. In other words, talk with him/her and not about him/her.

☙

Provide personal items whenever possible.

☙

Buy them their favorite foods.

☙

Provide music that pleases them.

☙

Make a scrapbook for them to look at that is filled with pictures and reminders of them at their healthiest best.

☙

Remember to practice the Golden Rule:
"You shall love your neighbor as yourself."

☙

Ask, "How would I want to be treated in this circumstance?"

☙

Questions to Consider:

What is your definition of dignity?

❧

What do I want my end of life to look like? Sound like?
Physically feel like? Smell like? Taste like?
Emotionally feel like?

❧

How can I provide the greatest dignity and sense of
empowerment to my loved ones?

❧

What qualities does this loved one have that I want to honor?
How do I, how can I, live those in my own life?

❧

*I'm tired of all this isolation. I'm tired of this triviality of life.
I want real human emotion. I want to feel the natural spontaneity of life,
the beautiful randomness and rawness that is life. I want to see you
and I want you to see me and I want to bask in that moment of humility and
intimacy and the acknowledgement of your dignity and my humanity,
even if it is for a second.
That'll be enough"*

~ Kate Miller ~

Faith

What the caterpillar calls the end of the world,
the master calls a butterfly.

~ Richard Bach ~

Even if we have lived a life of kindness and caring and have been involved with our faith of choice, we may experience great fear at the time of our death. Dying is the ultimate leap of faith! Death is beyond knowing, beyond knowledge.

What exactly waits for us? The answers vary, according to different religions and beliefs. Many, while in the dying process, may question their previous beliefs. How many of us willingly step into the unknown?

Our faith may be personal or may be public. We may take great comfort in our personal faith or we may be filled with questions or anxiety. What we believe about our own death can make the difference from departing with ease or lingering in fear.

End of life is a crucial time to listen, respect our possible differences in faith, and to love.

.

When my son Michael was twelve years old, he wrote me this poem:

> My mother is a woman who likes things done her way.
>
> My mother is a woman who works hard every day.
>
> She thinks of others with very kind thoughts and I know that others like her lots.
>
> She has her ways and I have mine and as you can see we are two of a kind.
>
> I know I am growing up very fast and soon everything will have been in the past.
>
> But there is one thing that will never part and that is mine and my mother's heart.

When Michael was eighteen, he went away to college and began making his own way. It was at this time that I also finished my college education and began making my own life, flying solo.

During the next several years as Michael and I followed our separate paths, our hearts seemed to grow closer. He traveled in his work and would invite me to each new city. He taught me about "stepping out of my box." His generosity and encouragement opened my heart and mind to the callings of my soul. Like Jonathan Livingston Seagull, Michael encouraged me to fly beyond my own self-imposed boundaries while he also championed my accomplishments as a woman.

Faith

As a child, Michael was "under my wing." Now, my child was the wind beneath my wings.

When Michael was thirty he was found to have a terminal disease, which he lived with over the course of five years. This story is about his amazing grace and how his inspiring process of living and dying breathed new life into me.

When Michael told me of his disease, I felt like something in me was dying. He showed me, by his own example, how miracles happen by facing pain. He led me to acknowledge my pain and to dare to talk about things that we had never confronted before. The healing comes when that painful place is filled with joy. From this I learned that it is not about waiting for the storm to pass; it is about learning to "dance in the rain."

My son taught me to walk through my fears, to accept, to love, and to honor the truth of my soul.

During those years, Michael breathed new life into me until I once again was able to take my child back "under my wing." My faith and my relationship with my son kept me going. We made more, and then more, precious memories together. Then, one April morning as the sun was coming up, Michael began to tell me of the visions he was having about a beautiful, emerald green place. It was then my own spirit of grace that led me to know it was my time to release him, to give my son permission to let go of his physical body and to breathe in the new life.

And, so it was, the "passing it forward" with my son's amazing grace rebirthing me and my part in rebirthing my son.

Michael died that night. As I stood beside his bed, he spoke these words, "Mom, the air is so fresh and everything is so green." I knew he was at peace on his new path with his new life in his pristine, emerald forest. I spoke the names of each family member and spoke these words over and over, "We love you, Michael."

I knew my son was now in the arms of pure love and that divine presence would be with him always.

Sometimes we may just need to remind one another of the best of our faith.

*M*ary lived her passion for life, her passion for peace, her passion for all that brings good to the world. A Quaker, she was a 4'11", ninety-pound ball of energy. She never married, but had many "children" during her career as a teacher. Upon her retirement, she moved back to her family home, and the neighborhood children were blessed with her commitment to expand their world. She would walk two miles to the local library to have books to read to them after school and taught them how to make music on her piano.

Faith

At ninety-one, Mary was still politically active and wrote her legislators about peace and justice issues on a weekly basis. When she became ill, she hand wrote her letters and asked me to type and mail them for her. As her illness progressed, she was hospitalized. On our last visit, I was surprised when I entered her room and saw how feeble and weak she had become. Each breath was labored. I sat beside her on her bed and took her thin, frail hand, gently holding and caressing it.

In my mind, I said, It is okay to let go, Mary. She looked at me and responded out loud, "Think life, not death, Liza." I again, only with my thoughts, said, That is life, Mary. I looked back into her eyes and saw the depth of her faith and her love. She responded, "We don't need words to talk, do we?"

"No we don't," I answered and gently kissed her cheek.

That night, after a dear friend had come to say his goodbye, Mary left her well-used body, moving onto the life where once again her spirit could soar with ease to her beautiful music.

*Faith is a knowledge within the heart,
beyond the reach of proof.*

~ Kahlil Gibran ~

*H*aving been blessed with being there when many have died, I encourage everyone I know to be there with their loved ones when they pass on. There is often a physical change in their countenance, and it becomes clearly visible when they leave their body. Peace is apparent on their faces.

Marian, who died of cancer in her mid-thirties, profoundly exhibited this contentment, and it was caught on camera. She had been sent home with hospice care and had been unconscious for weeks. Within a day after her son's birthday, she took a noticeable turn for the worse. I was at work when her husband called and asked me to come home because he thought it was "time." Being Vietnamese, their culture was different than I was accustomed to, but I had promised to be there to help with everything because of his language barrier.

When I entered the room, her breathing was labored with breaths several seconds apart. As I scanned the surroundings, I noticed a video camera on a tripod near the bed with the record light on. Her husband explained he wanted to capture this time because the children (first and fifth graders at the time) and other family members were not there, and they would want this record to remember her. I respected his wishes and stayed with them both as she passed. Once her breathing had stopped completely, he asked me several times if she was dead, and I just looked at him without responding. Then we both saw the moment when she let go.

Faith

At that time I turned to him and nodded as tears were streaming down both of our faces.

I excused myself from the room, called the hospice number and went to pick up the children from school. When I brought their children home, they went in to see their mother and were not afraid. In fact, they watched the video shortly after and saw the same magical moment we had seen.

Since this time I continue to encourage others to be there at this special time. Many are scared and cannot truly understand my request, but another close friend took my advice and stayed in the room with her husband while he died. Afterward, she thanked me numerous times for giving her the best gift ever, a chance to see the peace in her husband's face as he passed into the next world. Witnessing this moment gives you the strength to deal with the tasks ahead and the comfort to know your loved one is in a wonderful place. What a blessing it is to be a witness to seeing them smile at you as they let go of your hand and grab onto the hands of those on the other side.

*As your faith is strengthened you will find that there is no longer the need
to have a sense of control, that things will flow as they will,
and that you will flow with them,
to your great delight and benefit.*

~ Emmanuel Teney ~

My grandmother had been relatively healthy and took a turn downhill just a few weeks before her death. She was eighty-nine years old and had admitted to being "very tired" and ready to move on to the next place. As her nature was to be extremely stubborn, she kept that character throughout her life here on earth. She refused to eat or receive medication in order to speed up the dying process. There were several one-sided conversations between her and family members who had gone before her, which seemed to make her content.

    I had chosen to spend time with her during her final hours and took the opportunity to reassure her that we would all be fine, and she should feel free to let go and trust me to take care of the family. I held her hand and felt the life move from her body as I continued to let her know she was loved and would never be alone. As she began to slip away, she squeezed my hand one last time and I saw three teardrops fall from her right eye down her cheek. I could sense her waving goodbye as she let go and took my grandfather's hand!

Faith

Faith will move mountains.

~ Proverb ~

My thirty-five year old artist friend was dying from a fast-growing cancer. The doctors could not understand how he was still alive as lab results and x-rays indicated that he should have been dead days before. But his body was young, athletic and strong.

The hours stretched into days, which passed into weeks, which turned into months. He was ready to go but was not having any success. He was in great pain, and it was finally agreed that he could have as much pain killer as was needed to control his pain, even if that turned out to be a lethal dose.

There were eight or nine of us in the hospital room with him, including his doctor. His voice had become soft, and we listened carefully to his words. He told us of a door that wasn't exactly a door, but it was made of light, and he decided to go through it. Then, he described a circle of angels, which was not a common image in his New York Jewish upbringing!

In a moment he said, with the biggest grin on his face, "I don't know what kind of flowers these are," and then "Whoa, I don't even know these colors!"

With that, he stopped breathing. Almost immediately, a fine diaphanous mist drifted up from him, across from him and out the window. I wrote off the vision of this to my fatigue. After everyone said their final goodbyes, we all just sat with him for an hour or so.

As the sun was coming up we all decided to go to breakfast. I was floored when someone at the breakfast table brought up the mist, or whatever it was, that I saw lift up and out of his body. We were stunned as one after another said that they had seen it as well, yet most of them, like me, had blamed fatigue. And the greatest gift of all was his final big, beaming grin.

One of the greatest gifts we can give people is the hope that their death is nothing to fear-- you know, not that it has no fear in it, but the promise of scripture is that God will lead us through the valley of the shadow of death.

~ Max Lucado ~

Faith

My maternal grandmother, my last living grandparent, had been tired and "ready to go" for several years before her time came. My grandfather was gone, and she was lonely and full of the aches and pains of an eighty-seven year-old body. She had always been quite feisty and ready to give her opinions about everything from the neighbors to politics. Now, she didn't even have the strength for political banter.

Grandma could no longer bake the special holiday treats that used to bring her such joy in serving her twenty-two grandkids and our families. Her arthritis made it too painful. I believe it was Christmas 2003 that I baked some of the special coffee cakes from her recipes, along with lots of other goodies, and took pictures and sent them to her. I was so proud that they turned out "almost as good" as hers!

That ended up being her last Christmas. She got sick the following summer with intestinal problems, blockages and other ailments on top of the heart problems and arthritis. This time she really was ready to go. When Mom called to tell me Grandma was in the hospital, I wasn't sure if I should go home to Chicago to see her or if the hospital stay would be over soon, and we'd all see her at Christmas. Mom called again from the hospital, and I got to talk to Grandma.

She was facing surgery for removal of the intestinal blockage and was having a hard time deciding if she wanted surgery or not. She sounded tired and scared. I remember telling her that she would have to make that decision and nobody could really tell her what to do. I told her that I loved her, and she returned the sentiment. That was when I decided I needed to go home to see her one last time. I flew home the following Saturday, a few days after Grandma's surgery. She was not doing well. My mother and her four siblings were at Grandma's bedside. I was on the plane looking out the window, wondering if I would get there before she was gone.

Looking at the clouds and the blue sky around them, I thought about heaven and what Grandma's image of it might be. I knew she would be released from all of her pain and that gave me comfort. When Dad picked me up at the airport, he gave me the news. Grandma had passed about an hour ago, as I was looking out the window thinking about her, clouds and heaven. I didn't get there on time.

Over the next few days, one by one, all of the grandchildren and great grandchildren arrived to say final goodbyes at the funeral. Family "reunions" at funerals are strange, bittersweet times. We'd all talk and laugh and catch up with each other, then pause for the sadness of the reason we are there. It's part of the circle of life. Somehow the sadness is transcended, and we celebrate the spirit of family bonds. We are thankful for having had a wonderful Grandmother in our life who was our example of family love.

The evening after the funeral, I flew to Sedona for a meditation retreat that had been on my calendar for several months. I was tired and feeling altitude sickness creeping in as I made the two-hour drive from the Phoenix airport to Sedona. The next day, as I slowly walked the medicine wheel path and tried to center myself, I looked up to the clouds, and there was an eagle soaring. Grandma had come to say goodbye.

"Come to the edge," he said.
They said, "We are afraid."
"Come to the edge," he said.
They came.
He pushed them...
And they flew.

~ Peter McWilliams ~

Acts of Faith:

Listen to their fears, without discounting or minimizing. Acknowledge that you hear their concerns.

☙

Ask if there is a minister or spiritual leader with whom they would like to talk with. Arrange for a meeting.

☙

Ask if you can read to them from their sacred text of choice.

☙

Play music or a relaxation tape that will remind them of love, kindness, compassion.

☙

Share personal stories of your shared history that will remind them of their goodness.

☙

Faith

Questions to Consider:

What are my faith beliefs regarding death?

☙

What are my fears?

☙

How comfortable am I with the unknown?

☙

When have I experienced times of being with the unknown with ease? What helped me?

☙

Who is someone I can talk with to answer my questions and/or remind me of my faith?

☙

What sacred texts or readings support me in my faith understanding?

☙

Letting Go

When it comes time to die, be not like those
whose hearts are filled with the fear of death,
so when their time comes they weep and pray for a little more time
to live their lives over again in a different way.
Sing your death song, and die like a hero going home.

~ Chief Aupumut, Mohican ~

Being with others as they let go, supporting them in the process of dying, can actually provide a deep healing within ourselves. Our culture does not usually support grief. If you think back to your first exposure to grief, you were probably a child surrounded by adults who were distressed. Often the distress is cloaked in secrecy and confusion. The adults that you relied upon for safety may not have been readily available emotionally and physically. We decided early in our life that grief is scary and is something to avoid at all cost. Since we avoid it, we don't know how to grieve. We suppress, we deny.

Add to that the fact that death in our culture, at this time in history, has become something distant from us and unknown. With the advent of CPR and technology to keep us alive, death is delayed and prolonged. Our sick and elderly now are separated from us by hospitals and nursing facilities. Professionals provide the care.

How does this impact our ability to be with our loved ones at the time of their passing? It may feel as if we are stepping into a void of unknown, with no life jacket. We, as humans, have been known to stay in horrific situations rather than let go into the unknown and experience grief over the loss of the known.

Instead of staying in fear, what if we ask ourselves, "What am I getting from hanging on?" This confusion and pain can be our work to do, rather than our imposing it on our loved ones. We can ask, "How can I best love this person? "

*G*ranny was the best. She loved with joy, a listening heart, a generous spirit, and unconditional acceptance. Even into her nineties, she maintained an innocence. I am deeply grateful that she was my daughter's grandmother. My daughters will never know a love exactly like that again. Here was a woman who was a part of their lives from the day of their birth. Here was a woman who would respond with joy at their triumphs and bolster them at moments of "defeat." She had been part of their fiber, in every way, their entire lives. How can anyone else fill that void?

No one can. What my daughters can do, however, is live those precious qualities with and for others. They can put fresh flowers in a Kentucky Fried Chicken bucket, her favorite meal, at the sign-in desk at her memorial service, bringing laughter to those who came to remember her. They can be her living legacy of joy and purity. They can love deeply. And as they do so, they can smile with remembrance of her.

Mystery seems to have the power to comfort, to offer hope,
and to lend meaning in times of loss and pain.
In surprising ways it is the mysterious that strengthens us at such times.
I used to try to offer people certainty in times which were not at all certain
and could not make certain.
I now just offer my companionship and share my sense of mystery,
of the possible, of wonder.

~ Rachel Naomi Remen, M.D. ~

Kathleen, Eleanor, and I had all worked together as friends at a small southern liberal arts college for most of our collective professional lives when Kathleen, the youngest of the three of us, surprised us all with a diagnosis of breast cancer. Twenty years of friends rallied around her with books, music, dinners, laughter, and support as she entered chemotherapy, lost her hair, and continued to work diligently. Throughout her treatment she maintained her signature positive attitude, she took care of herself, and she never lost her concern for those around her or slid into pathos.

More often than not, Kathleen was the encourager, the listener, the problem solver, and the stable presence. So when, after a year, the doctor pronounced the cancer in remission, all of us prayed a large thank you and prepared to move forward with her at our side, both personally and professionally, certain that she had a healthy number of years left in her life with us. Eleanor and I breathed a joint sigh that we had not had to use any of our worst-case scenarios and the three of us settled into our familiar, warm, and lively friendship.

However, life turned out to be not quite so orderly when, within the year, Kathleen received a second diagnosis of stage four ovarian cancer. Since stage five is death, all of us, including Kathleen, understood that her condition was dire. However, from the outset, she faced the intensive chemotherapy and prognosis again with honesty, humor, and resilience.

I'll never forget Christmas when she greeted Eleanor and me at her front door, bald as a cue ball, no eyebrows, huge blue eyes and Rudolph antlers sitting atop her shining head! "Merry Christmas," she grinned as we fell down laughing. And our trip to the wig and turban store will remain as one of the most hilarious times we shared as friends. As she tried on each wig, the three of us sang and joked and poked fun, bringing everyone in the store into our circle of laughter. In the end, black-haired Kathleen sported a red-haired wig. "If you're going to wear a wig," she quipped, "you may as well have everyone notice it!"

Even in the really hard times, Kathleen would only allow herself fleeting complaints, followed by, "It does no good to complain. Never mind."

Although Kathleen led a highly functional life over the two years and two courses of chemotherapy, in time the disease suddenly took over her body. In her characteristic and brave honesty, she met death with the same engagement that she had met life. Eleanor and I moved into the tasks required for our dear friend, helped her make decisions, stayed with her, laughed, cried, learned to attach a feeding tube, whatever was required to help her in her last month.

We stood around her bed with Kathleen's sister and the hospice nurse, all holding hands, laughing over stories, crying for the loss of our dear companion. Pensive and tender, Kathleen died.

When the nurse announced her departure, we all still felt her presence and knew that she hovered with us some moments longer in the room. She was now more light and energy than body.

When the college chaplain talked to Kathleen's friends and family to glean stories for her memorial celebration, he heard the same three things from nearly everyone who spoke about Kathleen's life. First, they said, she lived as a consummate professional. She worked with her whole heart and soul and was dedicated to the students she served. Second, she had a laugh that you could hear above all other sounds. It began deep in her belly and rose through her heart to escape full-bodied and robust through her mouth. Her laugh made you join in for the sheer joy of hearing it. And third, Kathleen never spoke ill of anyone; she practiced the high art of non-judgment daily, impeccably.

I miss my friend daily. So in her honor, I have taken her three legacies, heart-centered meaningful work, joyful laughter, and being non-judgment into my life as my daily practice. Each time I make a choice for joy, I hear her laugh rising on the air. Each time I choose non-judgment and expansive thinking around others' actions, I see her kind smile and soft eyes. Each time I join my life to the good of the whole in my life's work, I feel her firm knowing inside my heart.

Kathleen died as she lived, engaged and whole to the end and now she lives in and through me until I pass on her legacy intertwined with mine.

Life shrinks or expands in proportion to one's courage.

~ Anais Nin ~

We care for the elderly in our private home. We took care of a wonderful Christian woman, eighty-four years old, who was in the last stages of Alzheimer's disease. She had no family left except a nephew who cared for her affairs. We became Francis' family. She lived with us for almost three years.

Francis loved music and, in her day, played the organ and piano and was a worldwide traveler. We kept music playing in her room at all times. The music would minister to us, as well as Francis, as we would sit with her and care for her needs.

The day came when we knew Francis was going to die. She had no one in her room but my husband and me. I crawled into her hospital bed and lay beside her. I comforted her, loved her, and told her that it was okay to go on and be with the Lord. I told her that she would hear Him say, "Well done, thou good and faithful servant."

I sang to her the words I knew from the beautiful music playing. I explained to her that just as she left her mother's womb to be born into this world, she would leave this world to be present with her Heavenly Father in heaven, who loved her so much He wanted her to be with Him now. She would have no more discomfort or pain.

Francis passed away in my arms and she looked beautiful. Her skin was soft, without a wrinkle. She was at peace. I am thankful for the privilege to have been with her and have held her close until she passed from this life unto the next.

My own mother passed away unexpectedly. She and dad went out to eat on a Friday night with some friends. I was staying with them in their home and doing her laundry when I got a call from my brother, who was at the hospital. He told me Mother had just died. She'd had a massive heart attack on the way home from the restaurant.

I never got to say goodbye to my own mother. I had no preparation. I appreciated being able to be with Francis. Being with her, and comforting her, was a healing balm.

Letting Go

*When we know love matters more than anything,
and we know that nothing else REALLY matters,
we move into the state of surrender.
Surrender does not diminish our power, it enhances it.*

~ Sara Paddison ~

Facing mortality on earth seems to be much more difficult for those remaining than those consciously aware of where they are going. Once you allow yourself to get past your grief and sorrow to see the magic of this moment you have complete serenity. I have not found anyone moving from today's world into the next who could explain it clearly, but each and every one of them definitely had a peace about their future destination.

Those remaining here on earth are, by far, more profoundly impacted by the passing of their loved one into the next life. I recall my grandmothers specifically speaking to their relatives and friends from their past who had gone before them and reconnecting to the safety of a friendly spirit as they transitioned. Many times this dialogue lasted for weeks before death. I have learned much about their lives, stories and conversations, and I will cherish this knowledge always.

Each time I experienced this it was truly amazing, and I, too, felt surrounded by loved ones by extension. In my mind, I pictured this time as letting go of the hand here on earth while reaching out for the one there in eternity. There is great comfort in knowing those we love are not alone in their journey; in fact, they have often been waiting years to be reunited with those in their past.

Joy and comfort have always enveloped me when I share this experience with a loved one who moves on to the next level.

We can love others in the dying process the same way we love them in the living process. We acknowledge the best of what the relationship brought to us and celebrate the shared gifts of our time together.

*A*sh, my adopted greyhound, and I are sitting on the back porch tonight. It has been a long, hot, summer and we are not even into August yet. A slight breeze comes across the yard, tossing my hair. At the same time the chimes hanging from the post near me begin to swing together making a soft rhythmic sound. My thoughts immediately turn to another summer a few years ago.

It also had been a hot and dry summer but my friend, Janie, sitting in the white rocker on the back porch, didn't seem to mind. She was rocking and reading a book that had her full attention. I was sitting on the steps next to her, working on some thoughts for a letter

I was writing. We had spent a large part of the day in the swimming pool. Summer in the South makes a pool a double delight. She had put her book down and gazed out across the water, a far away look on her face. I watched her out of the corner of my eye hoping the pain I felt did not show on my face. She turned, looked at me, and smiled.

Janie was dying. Or so the oncologist told her two years earlier. He predicted three mouths of life left. I smiled inside thinking, "Ah, he does not know my Janie." We had been friends for over sixty years, and I had met few people who enjoyed life as much as she did. Good or not so good, Janie was all for living each moment of each day fully.

We connected at our first meeting. Our shared sense of humor was our major asset. We had left others in our group looking somewhat confused at our outburst of giggles, spontaneous, and in unison. We never could explain it. It wasn't reasonable, at least not to the average brain. We had also shared our ration of tears in concert, but whatever the circumstances, the giggles usually ended the tête-à-tête.

Janie called me last summer to drive with her cross-country to drop off her little convertible for her granddaughter. She didn't say so, but I think she knew she would not need it much longer. This would be her last generous gift to her "baby." I was in Hawaii at the time and couldn't go. When I returned home, I was appalled at the thought of her traveling that distance alone, with her body full of chemo and radiation. She giggled my concern away and walked into the kitchen for another cup of coffee.

She told me that when she knew the time to leave this earth was near as she would take no more treatments. She saw no need in lingering. "Darling, this life has been a hell of a ride! I'm thankful for each and every one of the days I've had, so why drag it out?"

She left this planet in the springtime. Perfect… she was born on a day in spring. I always thought the idea of new birth, of life, loveliness everywhere, laughter, and birds singing were a perfect portrayal of her true nature.

We talked to each other at least once a day during her last stay in the hospital. We declared our love for each other, acknowledged our belief we would meet again, and sometimes we relived a happy memory together. I talked to her the night before she died. She was free of pain now. She was amused as she tried to explain to me the butterflies floating across her bed. Evidently she was trying to embrace one of the elusive "darlings" as she put it. Her last words to me were, "I love you." The next morning she was gone from the planet I lived on.

Letting Go

A tinkle from the chimes on my porch brought me back from sweet recollections, depositing me into the realism of today. These chimes were her last gift to me.

*Since we cannot change reality,
let us change the eyes which see reality.*

~ *Nikos Kazantzakis* ~

The last of the human freedoms is to choose one's attitudes.

~ *Victor Frankl* ~

Acts of Letting Go:

Tell them you love what they brought to your life.

≈

Ask them if there is anything they need
that you can do for them.

≈

Ask for what you want and need.

≈

Read about and understand the grief process.

≈

Write and rip. Write out everything you are thinking and feeling, with no editing or censoring. Keep writing until you are "done." Rip it up. Wash your hands.

≈

Questions to Consider:

How do I grieve?

✺

What am I getting from this person that I will miss the most?

✺

How can I get those needs met?

✺

What am I afraid of losing?

✺

How do I say goodbye?

✺

What qualities of this person do I want to carry on as his/her living legacy?

✺

Forgiveness

*We achieve inner health only through forgiveness –
the forgiveness not only of others but also of ourselves.*

~ Joshua Loth Liebman ~

I am convinced that forgiveness is the most important consideration at the end of our life, forgiveness to ourselves for our own mistakes and forgiveness to others for their mistakes.

While I held the hand of my most remarkable, kind, and compassionate ninety-eight year-old grandmother, tears ran down her cheeks as she said, "I can't die yet because I did not do what I was supposed to do with my life."

Another elderly woman said she couldn't die yet, although blind and completely bed-ridden for years, as she still holds onto bitterness towards her own mother's actions.

Another was finally able to start her releasing process after she was able to forgive a friend and a family member whom she felt had abused her kindness.

We, as human beings, can have such high and absurd expectations of one another and ourselves. Where did we get this notion of perfection? Why is it that we believe we should know how to do everything and with perfection?

This is a perspective that helps me. Being the frugal person that I am, I often try to do my home repairs myself. One day I was trying to do a plumbing repair without full knowledge or skill. I ended up calling in a professional. He pulled out a tool that I had never seen before. I asked him where I could get one and he said I could buy one at the local hardware store for $10. You can be sure that I bought one and used it many times since.

It would have made no sense for me to "beat myself up" for not having used that tool before when I didn't know it existed. Yet, that is what we do to ourselves all of the time. We beat others and ourselves up for using the only tools they/we have, thinking things should have been done differently.

A belief system that facilitates forgiveness for me is to remember that I have done and am doing the best I know how. It is remembering that others are doing the best they know how as well. Forgiveness does not mean condoning a negative behavior. It does not mean "anything goes." We can forgive and have boundaries. We can forgive and keep out all that is not loving and nurturing for us. Forgiveness means we are not allowing what someone else did or didn't do, or said or didn't say, to steal our peace.

When we hold onto anger and bitterness, it is as if a part of our energy is anchored in a previous time and place. If we think of our brain as a computer, it is as if we have left a computer program open. Although minimized, except when a memory or situation brings it to the forefront, it is still taking up our "disk space." It is not allowing us to be our best because it is always running in the background. It is always "running" in our heart.

A coworker was losing her father to the chronic physical effects of alcoholism. Knowing that I had worked in the field and might understand an affected family member's thinking, she shared that she did not know how to visit his deathbed for a goodbye. She wanted peace but was reliving terrifying memories and resentment. She wondered if she should share them and try to resolve her lifelong issues, maybe give him an opportunity to apologize. A catharsis. But what about the expectations of serenity based on a dying man's behavior? What wisdom was there in having expectations from one who had habitually let her down?

"Make a positive memory, just one, no matter how seemingly insignificant," I recommended. I suggested that she share with him and let that be enough. This was a goal she could fulfill without requiring anything from him.

Later, she expressed sincere gratitude, said that she had done as we discussed, and it had changed her life. She felt at peace to let him go and would remember something positive.

Death makes life change.

*Forgiveness does not change the past,
but it does enlarge the future.*

~ Paul Boese ~

Careening through yet another maze
    Sterile, posted, windowless hallways
Lead to a numbered room containing
Mother in childish gleeful repose.

I wonder at her enraptured gaze out the window
As she claps her gnarled hands and points
Chattering shiny black grackles swarming
A private rooftop show in late afternoon sun

Forgiveness

A roller coaster plight, she rests on a peak now,
Having made the sharp hairpin curve
Of last night's valley of oblivion.
Our seatbelts tightened, we hang on for the ride.

Much lighter now, her playful spirit soars
Complaints and pains all but a memory
Sweet warmth replaces past regrets
Flaring angers, lingering resentments slip away.

A deep breath of sadness circles through as I
Exhale memories of abandoned childhoods.
Trauma's shadow fades in the light of choice,
Free to be the Holy Mother we both missed.

A lifelong relationship of teaching and learning
True appreciation for the thrill of the ride.
Shared experience, genuine compassion
Caught now in love's perfect balance.

Forgiveness means letting go, now. Forgiveness means accepting the reality of the past. It means accepting mistakes. It means freedom to move onto the splendor of what is next.

*D*elores did not have a happy life. Her uncle and other males sexually abused her as a child. Her mother was emotionally abusive. Pregnant by a married man by the time she was sixteen, she married another who promised to help her but abused her instead. After bearing a child by him, he went to prison for killing a man, and she was on her own with two boys under the age of five. At the age of twenty-two, she decided to go to business school and took out a loan but never realized her goal. She was diagnosed with uterine cancer. She did her best to care for herself and her boys, but things were really bad. They ate oatmeal most of the time, and she couldn't seem to stop the pain and the bleeding. She thought she would die and worried about what would become of her boys.

That is when she met Jake. He lived in the same apartment building, and, no one really knows why, he took pity on this little family. He came one day with a box of donuts, winning the boy's hearts instantly! He offered to marry Delores so she would be on his insurance and be able to have the surgery she so desperately needed. She saw him as a knight in shining armor, and the boys couldn't see past the donuts.

It was good for a while, but happiness was not to be hers this time either. After years of abuse and finally divorce, she tried to make it on her own. She fell at her job waiting tables and hurt her back. A cousin told her about a doctor who would do surgery. He said she could sue the restaurant, make a bunch of money, and never have to work again. That did not happen. She got a small settlement, but now could not work, more due to the surgery than to the accident. She became addicted to pain medication and, over the years, required larger and stronger doses. Her addiction finally led to a morphine implant that released the deadly drug into her body at a steady pace.

She was in a daze most of the time. Her sons (now adults) tried to intervene at one point when they realized how bad she had become, but she cursed them and told them that she was an adult, and they couldn't tell her what to do. She had isolated herself, and her sons cooperated, not wanting to see her slowly killing herself and angry because she wouldn't stop. Then the day came.

The healthcare worker who helped care for Delores during the day called the oldest son and said she had found his mother unconscious in her chair and that she had been taken to the hospital. By the time we arrived, Delores was on life support, and the doctors had determined that she had taken other pain medication along with the morphine. Her brain was constantly seizing. They were giving her medication to stop the seizures, but they had to give her so much of it that they were afraid they were going to kill her with their efforts.

They approached the oldest son (my life partner) and told him that he would have to unplug the life-support. They couldn't do it. The family had a meeting, and it was decided that would be best, but so much had gone unsaid. There was so much anger. So many ugly things had been said. There was so much hurt that would never be mended. She would die with a broken heart, separated from her sons, never to tell them she loved them and that she was sorry. She was never to hear that they loved her.

Her oldest son unplugged the machine, holding back his sobs. The doctors said it would be quick, and she would die almost instantly, but she didn't. She lingered and she suffered. She would not go, not like that!

Finally, I took her hand. I told her that her sons loved her and always had, but that they just didn't know what to say or do so they stayed away. I told her that her boys knew that she loved them and told her some of the funny and loving stories that they had shared with me. The heart monitor slowed as I held her hand and told her that now it was time to end the pain.

She had suffered enough. I told her that all her family was there and that they all loved her and wanted her to be happy and to not worry about them. They understood.

She took a deep breath and slowly left her body. She was gone. She let go and was at peace at last.

*Sincere forgiveness isn't colored with expectations that
the other person apologize or change.
Don't worry whether or not they finally understand you.
Love them and release them.*

~ Sara Paddison ~

Acts of Forgiveness:

Make a list of everyone and everything that you have not forgiven. For each one, do the "Write and Rip" exercise of getting a blank piece of paper and write out all of your thoughts and feelings. Do not censor. Write it all out and keep writing until you feel complete. Rip it up and wash your hands.

Identify any belief systems you are holding in regard to the situation. Are any of them "stories" based on assumptions or from having taken things personally? Are they based on the falsehood of perfection? Identify the true facts, eliminating your stories. What are your new belief systems?

Identify the emotional, physical, social, and spiritual "costs" of holding onto your resentment and anger. Identify a new possibility in which you can reclaim your life of fullness.

Forgiveness

Walk a labyrinth, releasing any negative feelings.
(Many churches and retreat centers have labyrinths
open to the public.)

ಏ

Make a list of all of the qualities that you or the other person
have that you appreciate.

ಏ

Identify the gifts that have come into your life because of your
having had that particular experience
with that particular person.

ಏ

If your loved one is not feeling forgiven,
go back to the listening experience and remind him/her
that he/she is loved.

ಏ

Questions to Consider:

Who do you need to forgive?

☙

What do you need to forgive?

☙

What do you get from hanging on to un-forgiveness?

☙

What is the cost?

☙

What are new possibilities?

☙

What is a way you can get your needs met and forgive?

☙

Celebration Circles

Come out of the circle of time
And into the circle of love.

~ Rumi ~

How many times have you attended a memorial service and thought, "I wish _____ could have been here to hear all of the wonderful things said?"

Have you ever heard a loved one question the impact of his/her life? Do you sometimes question the impact of your own life?

During my year working in the nursing facility, I heard over and over the need to know that their life had been well lived. They needed to know others were touched in a meaningful way by their actions.

How do we know this? How do we truly and deeply "get" that we made a difference? There is such a disconnect in our world today. We rush, we do, we numb ourselves, through drugs (prescribed or not), television, work, shopping, computers. We forget to take the time for ourselves, much less for one another. We forget to tell others what they mean to us. We think, "I'll do that later."

What if you knew, deep into your toes and into every cell of your body that your life had mattered? What if you knew that others in your world, and maybe those you have never met, were different in a positive way, because you existed? What if you had the opportunity to learn that simple things you did had made an impact?

Imagine this: You are sitting in a circle of family and friends. You look around, one to one, and you see their smiles and you see their love.

It is pouring to you in their words, their laughter, and in their stories. They are saying things such as, "Because of you, I had this experience. Thank you."

"When you did this, it touched me."

"You modeled for me how to be this kind of person. Thank you."

"I honor you for what you brought to my world."

What if you created this opportunity for your loved ones? How would you like to create just such holy moments for someone else that touches everyone present in a profound way?

You need no money to do this. You need very little commitment of time. What you do need is to remember there is no "one right way" and to have the intent to make a difference.

I am on a mission.

I see the world covered in overlapping circles. Circles of love, kindness, gentleness, laughter, and deep healing. You are invited to join in the celebration.

Are you in?

Ready. Get set. Go!

Jerry was a Quaker, diagnosed with terminal cancer in his "midlife." As he was having a conversation with his wife and one of the friends from their spiritual community, he made the statement that he wished he could be present for his memorial service. That was all that needed to be said.

A "pre-memorial" was set in place. His comfortable easy chair was brought to the front of the worship room, and he was assisted to sit, facing the room filled with family and friends. There were so many folks present that there was standing room only, spilling into the corridor. In the tradition of Society of Friends service, those who so chose stood and spoke about their experience with Jerry.

The sharing started, moving from person to person, row to row. Each person shared how Jerry had touched his or her life. He learned how his acts of kindness, that were just a part of who he was, had unknowingly made an enormous impact on others. Everyone in the room was tremendously moved. His father-in-law of over thirty years said he learned things about Jerry that he had never known.

I visited Jerry at his home a short time afterwards. He was still glowing, with the knowing of how his life had mattered to so many. He was basking in the love he had received. One friend's act of grace brought this gift to Jerry and brought great meaning for all of us to witness.

A Celebration Circle may be an impromptu, one-on-one conversation. My grandmother, at ninety eight, was still of bright mind, but her body was used up. She could no longer tend to her needs. She could no longer walk or participate fully in life. During one of our last visits, with tear-filled eyes, she said, "I can't die yet as I didn't do what I was supposed to do."

I shared stories from my childhood, reminding her of the great love she had shared with me. I reminisced about the times she taught me how to gently tend a garden, how to create beautiful ceramic pieces, how she read to me, and played canasta and "button-button." I reminded her of the impact she had on me that has been passed on to my children and grandchildren.

Similarly, my aunt at ninety five, expressed her fears to me. She said she could not die until she did one more good thing, for one more person. She could not get out of her bed in the nursing facility. Her leg was twisted and atrophied, following a broken hip. She was adamant in needing to know she had been kind enough, to enough people. I shared my childhood memories with her and how I always looked forward to visits with her. Even though I was a child she always took the time to listen to me. She, as did my grandmother, would make a committed effort to participate in a craft project with me, teaching me something new each visit. She loved me as the daughter she had lost, many years earlier.

As a Native American healer, I share my gifts in many shapes and forms. One of the ways is to assist the elderly. One of my clients, an elderly Native American man, was bent with the ravages of arthritis. We talked at length about how he saw death and what happened to a person when they left here and where we thought they went. He accepted the thought that his life energy lived on after his body died.

One day he announced his body was "ready for the heap!"

"I do not want any fanfare and hoop-de-la for me. You know my kids don't give a hoot, so I say we have one for me while I am here and you can come and sit and admire me while I lay on the couch."

The next day I shaved him and dressed him in his suit and laid him on the couch. I sat for about ten minutes, admiring him and paying tribute. He sat up, laughed, and said "That's enough." He said he was sure glad we got that out of the way and told me I did a fine job admiring him. Winking, he said I ought to think about doing this for a living.

He was my friend and, in the end, I honored all he wished for. I know in my heart that he died happy.

This elder asked for what he wanted. The experience was not only meaningful for him, but for his friend. It was short. It was sweet. It was rich in meaning and depth. It was a Celebration Circle for two.

Are you seeing the infinite possibilities?

In talking about Celebration Circles with a minister, he shared that his church has many elderly members who can attend only sporadically because of fragile health. I suggested to him the idea of creating a culture in his church that when someone who wasn't able to attend regularly was able to come that there would be a spontaneous, "Let's form a circle." The person could request it him/herself, or another member could make the request. It could be a simple and easy sharing of stories and appreciation for that person. Or, in a Sunday School class there could be a rotation of each member being honored on a weekly or monthly basis, until all had the experience. If the honoree was announced in advance, family members could be invited. Such possibilities!

Another form of Celebration Circle can be with advance planning and by invitation only.

*F*rom an austere background and being the only daughter, Helen learned to be "tough." Although physically she is "just a slip" of a woman, her spirit belies her size. She is strong, willful, and gentle all wrapped up in one. Through her perseverance and her committed efforts, she made it through medical school when women were very much in the minority. She has made her mark. Her toughness against the male "establishment" has been beautifully mixed with the compassion and the gentleness of her female nature.

Being a physician, Helen knew right away when she exhibited symptoms of her cancer that it was serious. She made a conscious decision to mindfully and joyfully "walk through the shadow of death." She has served as a model for all who witness her attitude and her life.

Helen's Celebration Circle was held in the parlor of her church. The living-room-like setting was inviting with a couch, chairs, a table with fresh flowers, windows overlooking a garden area, and pictures on the wall. Her friend Melissa, who is also the Missions Director of the church, was pivotal in making arrangements and creating a beautiful experience. Helen had determined a "guest list" and I had mailed out invitations. Signs were put up on easels at central spots to guide guests to the parlor.

Chairs were arranged in a large circle, with Helen seated on the couch. After introductions, I modeled the sharing, keeping it short and lighthearted. As each person shared their stories and gratitude to Helen, s/he would move and sit beside Helen. A video camera was set up to capture the moments. With the invitation having an end time, as well as a beginning time, it helped to set the stage for consideration of allowing everyone an opportunity to share. Someone had brought a DVD with heart messages from friends

Helen had worked with on mission trips in Central America. These were shown with a TV and DVD player that was brought into the room. Kleenex sat on the coffee table, but was seldom used as mostly the room was filled with laughter.

Afterwards, everyone was invited to share in the offered water, lemonade, cookies, and mixed nuts. Informal conversations continued. A group picture was taken, later to be mailed out with a copy to each guest, along with a copy of the DVD.

Helen's comments summarized the experience perfectly, "It was a very wonderful, emotional, and fun time for me. Sometimes we wonder if we have made a difference in people's lives and it's good to hear others say that we have."

With disabling dementia, Mom is living in a structured environment. Although she still recognizes her children and grandchildren, for over two years she has been unable to be engaged in a conversation or make choices for herself. Imagine my surprise when, out of the blue, she was alert and even asked questions. Her face was bright and her memory improved. She requested to look at a family album, one of her previous favorite pastimes, and was even able to relate stories about the pictures.

It was time to act fast. I immediately contacted her grandchildren and cousins by e-mail. I informed them of Mom's condition and shared the concept of Celebration Circles. I offered some possible dates for gathering, knowing that because of the short notice and the geographic distances involved most could not attend. I suggested if they could not do so, they send a 2-3 minute video or a letter, sharing a story of an experience with Mom.

It was a small gathering of eight, including my two daughters, two cousins and spouses, and my friend who videoed the experience. We met in a group room that is available in her nursing facility, in the late morning as this is a time she is usually more energetic. We sat in a casual circle and told Mom what we appreciated about her. We laughed with the remembrance of the stories. We rotated reading the letters sent by others.

Due to her short attention span and her inability to sit still for an extended time, it was clear when it was time to end the sharing. I returned her to the "day room" and several family members joined her there to give her a farewell hug. She was able to relate best one on one. Although it was difficult to tell how much she understood, it was a precious time to remember and treasure.

Celebration Circles don't have to be related specifically to the end of life. Birthdays, holidays, and family reunions can all serve as opportunities to honor others.

My mother-in-law turned ninety a few months ago. Her daughter had arranged a luncheon party for her at a local women's club and invited about fifty close friends. She had been a nationally-ranked senior tennis player and among the guests were a high school friend, a college roommate and many decades-younger tennis players. All wanted to pay tribute to her at this momentous event.

After we ate, her daughter invited each of us to stand and share a story of how we knew the guest of honor and what she meant to us. Many had humorous stories, some of which had happened over fifty years ago. We each got to know her much better from anecdotes of neighbors, life-long friends and competitors. As every person spoke, we discovered a running thread – that she had baked almost every person in the room one of her famous pies over the course of these friendships.

It was a tremendous honor and great privilege to have been invited to this event and to have had the opportunity to publicly acknowledge her place in our lives, both to her and to others. I will never forget this event. To be able to have a group of friends and loved ones come together while a person is alive to hear the words of love and affection is very gratifying for everyone involved.

Do you see it? Do you see the circles forming, joining, bringing light, bringing awareness, bringing connection? Do you see a world joined in a communion of spirit? YOU are invited to this party. Please play with me!

*What cannot be achieved in one lifetime
will happen when one lifetime
is joined to another.*

~ Harold Kushner ~

Acts of Creating a Circle:

WHO:

Do you know someone who is nearing the end of his/her life?
Do you know someone who may be struggling and is in pain?
Do you know someone who could benefit from being reminded of their best?
Has someone made a difference in your life?

If the answer is yes to any of the above, you have the first step.

Who would you like to invite to be on your "team?" If you are feeling any discomfort in planning/ facilitating such a circle, who can you think of that can assist?

For example: a friend, a family member, a minister, a social worker/ counselor, or a hospice worker. For participation in action groups led by Liza, see www.centerofwellbeing.com.

WHAT:

What form do you want this to take?

Is it planned?

Is it spontaneous?

Is there an opportunity for others to participate remotely, via video phone calls?

WHEN:

When is this going to happen? Now, now, now, now, NOW! Have you ever procrastinated, or just not acted on a prompting, later to regret it? Have you ever missed a window of opportunity? Have you ever felt a sense of urgency or a gentle internal nudge to act that you ignored? Did you regret it later?

It is always the perfect time to express love!

That said, there are logistical considerations. What time of the day is the person honored most energetic? Is there a particular time in a course of treatment that would be best? Is s/he deteriorating in mind/ body/spirit quickly?

The answer as to "when" is to make it as comfortable and as easy as possible for the honoree.

WHERE:

    In the home

    In a church

    In a nursing facility

    In an assisted living facility

    Outside in a park

    In a friend's home

    Wherever everyone can be comfortable

HOW:

    Spontaneous

    Planned

    Two of us

    More of us

    Send out invites through the postal service

    Call

    E-mail

    Provide snacks, drinks

    Shared meal, pot luck, catered

        Are you getting there is no one right answer?
                          Just do it!

In the course of reading this chapter, have you thought of any particular friends, loved ones, acquaintances. Who are they? I invite you to write their names down now. Stop reading and write. Now, now, now, now, NOW!

For a worksheet designed to assist with planning the event, go to www.centerofwellbeing.com/publications and download the PDF file.

Questions to Consider:

Why would I want to be a part of a Celebration Circle?

Do I see it as an opportunity to reach out to others, and possibly bring healing?

Who comes to my mind and heart as people I would like to honor in this manner?

What do I need in order to feel comfortable in initiating this process?

And Then Some

*Seeing death as the end of life is like seeing
the horizon as the end of the ocean.*

~ David Searls ~

In sending out an invitation for sharing of end-of-life stories, I received some experiences that happened after a loved one's passing. One of the expressed reasons that we are fearful of letting go is because we have a belief that when our loved one dies, that is the end of all contact. Yes, that is the end of contact with the physicality of the other person. And yet, these stories may remind us that there is more to us than our physical being.

*M*om left us suddenly and unexpectedly at sixty-nine years of age when my sister was twenty-six and I was thirty. We were all stunned, knowing our lives would be forever altered.

It had been a gift for my younger sister and me to witness the beauty of the love between our parents. Mom and Dad were best friends for over forty years, and Dad returned home to eat lunch with her every day. A vibrant and expressive man, our father played Dixieland in a band when he was overseas in WWII. That is actually how they met. He would sing "their song" to her, and she would cry every time. It was Perry Como's "And I Love Her So." It wasn't a big hit, so it wasn't on the radio often.

We all knew the first wedding anniversary following Mom's death would be exceptionally difficult. We arranged for all of us to share a special dinner out. To keep it from being too gut wrenching for my dad, we called a restaurant that we never visited before. Making the reservation for five, we picked up Dad and all entered the restaurant together. We walked to our table to discover it had been set for six, rather than the requested five. As we sat down, we all stopped in disbelief as this rare old song, "And I Love Her So," started playing over the loud speaker. We all knew she was with us. Happy anniversary, Mom.

My husband, Ewell, died over four years ago. I still miss him, but life does go on. Then there are times when I am suddenly hit with a thought, a smile, or something that reminds me of him. This overwhelming sadness descends upon me, and I cry at the drop of a hat. I had a day like that not long ago. Finally, I asked him to just give me a sign that he was still around me to help me get over this sadness.

The number three was his lucky number. He always chose number three. His favorite race car driver was number three, Dale Earnhardt. When I went to bed on this particular night, I cried some more before falling asleep on my left side. Into the morning I felt a rough tug on my right shoulder. I tried to ignore it because I was comfortable, but I felt it again. Finally I turned over just in time to see the time. It was 3:33 AM. I said, "Thank you," and was deeply comforted by his message.

Although not all of the time, I know Ewell is still around me. When I need to know that there's more to death than just being gone, he comes through for me.

When my beloved husband died suddenly, I could still feel his spiritual presence for several months. In life, he would often come up behind me and wrap his arms around my waist in a big hug. I could still feel the energy of those hugs.

He and I had been in the process of planning a couple's retreat, and one of the exercises we were going to include was a "mirroring" experience. The couples sit or stand, face to face, and hold their hands out toward their partner, palms up and out so that their hands are touching. They then close their eyes, move their hands a couple of inches apart and the "leader" starts to slowly move his/her hands. The partner is sensitive to the warmth and energy, and the other's hands follow the movement, so the four hands dance in the air in unison. Being totally present to your partner, you can feel and move together.

At the times I would feel such deep despair and grief, I would hold up my hands into the air in front of my face with palms out and feel Austin's energy. Our hands would move in unison. It was such a comfort and reminder that his presence was not gone.

On our wedding anniversary, six months after his death, I was in the forest by our favorite tree where we had renewed our vows on one of our anniversaries. Tears were pouring down my face, wishing for his presence. I put up my hands and could feel that he was there. I then "heard" from him that it was time to let him go, that his mission on earth was finished but that mine wasn't. Suddenly, my hands swished to my extreme right, and he was gone.

He comes back for occasional visits, for dances, for encouragement and reminding. I smile with the remembrance of the beauty of his soul.

*M*y husband, best friend, lover, and business partner had died and left me. The grief was deep, long, and touched every area of my life.

One night I was on vacation, camping alone in the mountains of New Mexico. I had an exceptionally vivid dream that Lee had returned to my life. But he was across the room from me and would not come close and stand next to me. I asked him to join me, and his reply was, "I cannot be here for you like that anymore." I felt such heaviness and sadness as I woke up. Lying there, I then felt his arms wrapped around me as he lay beside me. He whispered in my ear, "You will love like this again." He was then gone.

His words have been a comfort to me. I believe him and know that my loving another would never diminish what we had together.

*M*y sister has often asked me how I can be so calm during times of death, most specifically when we lost our mother so unexpectedly. I explained to her the first feeling I had was being grateful that our mother was finally at rest and did not have to struggle with the confines of life on earth any longer. Second, I have found it to be selfish to become so absorbed in grief that you lose sight of the blessing this transition is for those leaving.

My belief is that these loved ones are only leaving us physically and not spiritually or emotionally. Several times immediately following her death, my mother came to help us identify her cause of death and gave me messages to pass on to my father and sister to ease their sadness. It is clear, she is still with us each and every day; we just have to look past ourselves and receive her without fear or reservation.

*M*y brother Stan died of ALS (Lou Gehrig's disease) in 1999 at the age of fifty-five. It was, in many ways, an awful death. Stan's incisive and argumentative mind seemed unaffected, but his ability to communicate faded away bit by bit, to nothing, to zero.

How that must have been for him I cannot, or perhaps dare not, imagine.

He and his wife, Noella, did a lot of crying together when they learned that the physical problems he began to notice in 1998 were the result of a degenerative nerve disease for which there is no cure. At the end of his life, he had lost every bit of muscle control. He could no longer smile or even blink.

And yet there were positive aspects to this slow departure from this life, including the chance he had to say full goodbyes. He found ways, even in his last days, to be generous to others, and he expressed to Noella surprise at discovering how many people knew, respected, and even loved him.

Although reluctant to do so, Stan chose to accept life-support systems so that he could live to see his son Reed graduate from high school. He had to be carried into the auditorium, but he was there on Commencement Day, a proud father.

For many years, Stan's spiritual life had been deepened by meditation training and involvement in a Boston-area Buddhist community based on the teachings of Chogyam Trungpa. He led me, Noella, and Reed into Shambala training also. This community was extraordinarily helpful, attentive, and faithful throughout the months of Stan's illness.

Buddhism suited Stan in being both non-theistic and open to the possibility of experiences beyond what we ordinarily consider to be real. In his philosophy of science work he sought to demonstrate that the scientific method, while extraordinarily useful, cannot claim certainty or determine the limits of what is real.

Stan believed, as I do, that reality is much more complex and less well understood than we usually assume. He wrote, for example: "A better understanding of spiritual influence on the body will make for better medical practice (which is to say) for better science. To take spiritual concepts into account in the practice of science is not to abandon science. To refuse to do so is to fall prey to an epistemological mistake."

Once in our younger years and then again after Stan knew his disease was terminal, he and I agreed that, if possible, the one of us who died first would attempt to make contact from "the other side." A month or more after my last visit with Stan, I was back in Houston when, I believe, he followed through on this promise. By then, he had been at the edge of death for at least two months, unable to communicate and being kept alive by machines. More than once, his doctor had told Noella to expect his death within a week, but they'd been wrong.

One morning in November 1999, I woke up from a powerful dream and immediately described it in detail to my wife, Kristi. In the dream I was sobbing because I knew Stan had just died. Then, also in the dream, I saw a woman sitting at a desk, holding a piece of paper, and she told me, "I have a message for you from Stan." I asked what it said, and she read from the paper, "There are many among you and multitudes more coming." Then I saw a male figure and, standing behind him, someone who did not look angelic in the standard sense, but who seemed ethereal and protective. In the far background of the dream, hazy figures seemed to be moving forward.

Kristi and I got up and went to a gym to work out. When we returned a couple of hours later, we had a message on our answering machine from Noella. In a tired and resigned voice, she said that Stan had ceased to be responsive and the life support systems would be removed the following day. For at least fifty other mornings that message would have come as no surprise. It came on the morning of the dream I've just described.

Over the years, I have gone from a childhood belief in life after death to a rejection of the idea as wish fulfillment, then to a sort of militant agnosticism..."I don't know and you don't either". Atheists and religious dogmatists, I believe, make a mirror-image error in claiming to know what cannot be known. I don't claim certainty about the meaning of my dream. I can't claim to know what it means.

But here is what I think. I think Stan was able to fulfill his promise to me and that the communication was successful. I think he communicated from the "other side" with words and symbols I could understand and that the message they conveyed is an encouraging one indeed.

Stan's slow, bit-by-bit death has given me an intensified awareness of the simplest aspects of being alive - tasting, smelling, seeing, touching another's face with our fingers, walking, drawing in breath. Stan's death showed me that what is most fundamental about being alive is exquisite.

His post-death message to me tells me that we are part of a caring creation, that life is not based only on chance. From my best male friend and brother, I take this message … our relationships, whether long-term or brief, matter profoundly now and, most likely, beyond life as we know it.

One of the songs Michael requested be sung at his celebration of life ceremony included the words, "Happy trails to you, until we meet again." A few years later, I had one of my fondest experiences of meeting again with Michael's joy-filled spirit. I was revisiting San Francisco where Michael and I had once spent a fun-filled holiday. I was sitting in a coffee shop in Haight Asbury, looking out the window. A young man stood tall in the middle of the sidewalk, with a white gift box held open in his hands.

Without my mind seeming to notice, my feet and legs moved me towards the young man and the box. I bent my head to see what was inside. My eyes saw clouds, billowy white at first, then as they seemed to come into focus, I saw flowers.

The young man, without a word, turned full body towards me and held the box invitingly for me to take a flower. I chose one and as my hands brought it to my nose to smell it's sweet fragrance, my eyes and head lifted as if by some unknown force so that my eyes met the young man's eyes.

We both stood there, gazing at one another. His soft eyes seemed to hold a message, telling me something. There seemed to be no expectation for money. I said, "Thank you," not being sure that I was thanking him for the flower as it felt I had been given much more.

I stood silent and still as he turned and watched his tall proud body walk with the box held closed in his hands as if his mission was complete. He never opened the box or offered the contents to anyone else and disappeared around the corner.

Not knowing why, I held this flower in my hand like something so precious I couldn't harm it, and I walked back into the coffee shop. The fragrance of the flower was exceptional. People began to ask me, "Where did you get it?" They seemed as enchanted by the flower as I was. When I would tell them who gave it to me, they were so surprised that someone would love these flowers and be giving them away.

They asked, "Where did he go?" They seemed in disbelief that such a thing could happen.

I was surprised at their responses because I thought this would be the most usual thing in the world for someone to be giving away flowers in the most known place in the country for love, peace, and "flower children."

The gift lives on in the flower to be held sacred in my hand and heart. It would be so like my son Michael to so delicately know and remind me that I am entitled to the best. Was this the message so silently given to me in the young man's eyes?

*T*his story starts on a restless Sunday afternoon when just a short drive in the country found me close to the lake and turning onto a dead end road. I was drawn to the small, redwood frame house in front of me, and I saw a big garden and a little shed out back as I parked my car. Someone was in the front yard, hammering a "for sale" sign in the ground.

I knocked on the front door and was welcomed by a voice saying, "Come inside." Mr. and Mrs. Absolute Sweetness were sitting in their matching chairs. They had been together so long, and you could just tell that they were still very much in love. I remember him being tall and handsome, almost ninety. She looked as if at one time she was small and dainty, and now just a little round and beautiful. Their love made them beautiful, for each other, their children, their grandchildren, and their home. The love between them was so palpable you could almost touch it.

It turns out they were selling their home to move in with their daughter who lived only a half mile down the road. Celebrating their seventieth anniversary had proven to be a little too much for them, so they had finally given into the wishes of their five children and many grandchildren.

I gave them a verbal and written contract that very day, knowing I wanted to buy the house based on the love I felt during the visit.

Later I discovered it didn't have a bathtub, and it needed many repairs. Yet, I was happy and peaceful there and resolved to love my new and only home as much as they had.

Six months later, Mr. Absolute Sweetness died. Tons of cars descended on the little lake road where we lived. I felt sad for his wife, wondering how she would go on now without him.

Mr. Absolute Sweetness had decided not to leave completely, not just yet. While his family was down the road, putting his body in the ground, it seemed he was up at my house in Spirit form. This was the house he and his wife had shared, and I suppose he was waiting for her, or perhaps, just checking in now and then from Heaven.

I heard his voice. He would close my doors for me and turn my lights on and off. I was not afraid. I felt comfortable with him being around because, for the first time, I was not alone. His presence was actually a comfort to me. When I would sense his Spirit pop in or when he would mess with the lights or doors, I would speak to him out loud. I knew he was just waiting for her, his wife of seventy years. I believe we helped each other in many ways as we coexisted.

After a year of living in his home, something simply amazing happened that changed everything for Mr. Sweetness and myself.

I was tired, restless and went to bed early about 9:00 PM. Although I was sleepy, sleep just would not come. I got up with warm milk and the current book I was reading. I suddenly felt lonely, put down the book, finished my milk, and crawled into bed. I fell into a deep and peaceful sleep.

Suddenly, I was wide-awake, and the bedroom was filled with swirling, effervescent, golden-silver light. I was immersed in it, surrounded by it, breathing it, floating in it. I was awed and amazed and, at the same time, knew I was safe. I felt to be in God's lap, complete and surrounded by love. Then I was asleep again.

As I was driving to work the next day, I noticed the daughter's house down the road had a funeral wreath on the door. I stopped, walked to the door, and knocked.

Mr. and Mrs. Sweetness' daughter came to the door. "My mother passed last night, around three."

True love is not to be denied. They shared their reunion with me, and for that I am forever grateful.

Questions to Consider:

What are my belief systems regarding what happens to us after our physical death?

～

How might I notice ways in which my loved one might still be present with and for me?

～

Death is not a period, but a comma in the story of life.

~ Amos Traver ~

Suggested uses for this book:

It is my hope that these stories of courage and inspiration gave you hope and expanded your way of being with "death." For us, as humans, to be able to accept and find ways to be with ourselves and others at the end of life could do wonders in reducing the current suffering in our world. I invite you to explore how you may use this book as a resource. Here are some possibilities:

You may choose to read each chapter on your own, answering the questions and exploring which activities will best serve your life. As circumstances change and other situations enter your life, I hope you will refer back to the suggested activities.

You may take the initiative for hospice support for your loved one. Often medical personnel are hesitant to suggest this option.

You may want to create your own Celebration Circles. See the support opportunities that Liza offers at
www.centerofwellbeing.com

☙

You may want to create a support group, or circle, to discuss and share together. This can be created from your network of friends, your church community, and/or your family.

Each chapter could be explored individually.

For a resource on how to create and support such a group, see *The Complete Guide to Small Group Ministry* by Rev. Bob Hill.

☙

You may choose to take the understanding from this reading into deeper action by forming a support group as defined in *Share the Care* by Cappy Capossela and Sheila Warnock, www.sharethecare.org.

☙

You may share your own conscious acts of grace stories by sending them to:
stories@giraffetalk.org

Appendix

This is a book of the heart. The reality is there are many legal and medical decisions to be made as well. Once the heart conversations are opened, it is my hope the more legalistic decisions, can be made with greater ease.

Spend time thinking about the kind of care you want or don't want and discuss your wishes with your family and loved ones. Then all that is left is to be with one another and experience the greatest possible peace in the last months or moments.

Here is a list of documents you may wish to consider to establish responsibility for personal affairs:

Last Will and Testament

Durable General Power of Attorney

Advance Directives, which may include:

A Living Will

Power of Attorney for Health Care

Do Not Resuscitate Order (DNR)

Depending upon your financial circumstances, you may also want to consider a Family Trust.

Knowing your wishes ahead of time can greatly reduce anxiety and suffering for everyone.

There are many resources on the web for each of these forms. In order to ensure all of your wishes are honored, please check out sources carefully and obtain appropriate legal counsel.

*When we ask ourselves
which persons in our lives mean the most to us,
we often find that it is those who can face the
reality of powerlessness...
and have chosen rather to share our pain,
and touch our wounds with a gentle and tender hand.
The friend who can be silent with us
in a moment of despair or confusion,
who can stay with us in an hour of grief and bereavement,
who can tolerate not knowing, not curing, not healing.*

~ Adapted from Henri Nouwen ~

To accompany this book, we recommend the meditation CD:

Breathe In Life

by Liza Ely and Dirje Smith

To play for the person you love who is in the dying process

❧

To open discussion with family members & medical personnel

❧

For yourself, as a reminder of the gift of releasing

❧

Anytime when relaxation is desired as a release from anxiety, sleeplessness, stress or fear

❧

Available as CD and as MP3 through
www.giraffetalk.org and
www.centerofwellbeing.com

www.ingramcontent.com/pod-product-compliance
Lightning Source LLC
Chambersburg PA
CBHW061653040426
42446CB00010B/1725